THE STUDY OF LATIN AMERICAN POLITICS IN UNIVERSITY PROGRAMS IN THE UNITED STATES

R. A. Gomez

THE UNIVERSITY OF ARIZONA

THE STUDY OF LATIN AMERICAN POLITICS
IN UNIVERSITY PROGRAMS IN
THE UNITED STATES

R. A. GOMEZ

THE INSTITUTE OF GOVERNMENT RESEARCH

Comparative Government Studies
Number 2

THE UNIVERSITY OF ARIZONA PRESS
Tucson, Arizona

THE INSTITUTE OF GOVERNMENT RESEARCH
The University of Arizona

The views expressed in this publication are those of the author and are not an expression of views of the Institute of Government Research or of the University of Arizona.

CONTENTS

FOREWORD

The study of Latin America in colleges and universities in this country is, as this survey reveals, a quite recent development. And so it is with political scientists studying the government, politics, and international relations of Latin American countries. In this volume Professor Gomez surveys the work of American political scientists with a Latin American specialty.

R. A. Gomez is a professor of Government at the University of Arizona. For many years he has specialized in Latin American government and politics. He is the author of *Government and Politics in Latin America* (New York: Random House, 1960; Rev. Ed., 1963). He has contributed to *The Americas*, the *Journal of Inter-American Studies, Inter-American Economic Affairs*, a chapter, "The Marxist Approach to Latin America," in *The Political Defense of Latin America* (Tempe: Bureau of Government Research, Arizona State University, 1963), and a chapter, "Peru: The Politics of Military Guardianship," in *Latin American Political Systems*, Martin Needler (ed.) (New York: Van Nostrand, 1964). Professor Gomez received a grant in 1961-62 from the Social Science Research Council for study in Peru, and from the American Philosophical Society for a study of Spanish migration to the United States.

This volume, the second in the Institute of Government Research Comparative Government Studies, will be of value to American students and teachers interested in Latin America, as well as to public and private agencies, in this country and abroad, which share that interest.

Currin V. Shields, Director
Institute of Government Research

INTRODUCTION

The study of Latin American politics in the United States now engages the attention of a sufficiently large number of professors and students to warrant appraisal as a "field" or at least as a widely practiced "specialty." Only a few years ago Latin Americanists among the great body of political scientists could be found only in that handful of universities which could boast of exceptional facilities for graduate work. Although many other professors elsewhere may have preferred Latin American research and teaching, they were engaged in those pursuits concurrently with a number of other interests which were usually in greater demand. In most smaller colleges and universities, the Latin American bent of a professor had to be liberally sandwiched into a broader course in international relations or comparative government. With the vast increase in student enrollments and the resulting increase of teaching staffs, separate courses in Latin American politics have mushroomed over the academic landscape. Many professors were able to strip away their secondary interests and, whether for good or ill, confine themselves entirely, or almost entirely, to Latin America. This Latin Americanist identity has been only one of the dramatic developments in those universities which have experienced incredible specializing trends in the years since the end of World War II. To have watched these trends has been to see some of the most wondrous curricular proliferations in that massive affair known as the American university system. In a department of political science of substance there can now be found not only a Latin Americanist but also a goodly number of "ists" from at least six other regions into which the comparative governmentalists have divided their universe.

1

Recent preoccupation with the developing systems around the world gave Latin Americanists a considerable boost, for any self-respecting student of Latin America has been nurturing that orientation for some time. A meaningfully broad classification within comparative government has emerged herein by means of which one can escape some of the older and more confining area classifications.

Since one of the reasons for our increasing interest in developing countries derives from the Cold War and the attempts of the United States and friends to prevent the spread of Communism into such allegedly fertile soil, Latin Americanists experienced a surge of popularity in that larger numbers of students sought positions in the foreign service or other national efforts such as aid programs, intelligence, information and the Peace Corps. The challenging subject of economic development has also led to greater specialization in the Latin American area.

Until quite recently, the number of books, articles and other publications dealing with Latin American politics, or closely related subjects, were few — in any language. There has been a very substantial output in the last five years. Not long ago, and to a considerable extent still, scholarly works were almost entirely publications that to some degree were drawn from doctoral dissertations. The first general textbooks on Latin American politics did not appear until after 1950. The author recalls that in his own graduate study (1946-48) Mary Williams' excellent 1945 edition of *The People and Politics of Latin America* was used as a basic text in both politics and history. There are now a large number of texts in politics and supplementary books touching on economic, sociological, historical and cultural aspects. A recent publication of the Hispanic Foundation of the Library of Congress (1964) lists 240 paperbacks now available on Latin American topics.[1]

---

1 Compiled by David H. Andrews; Edited by T. J. Hillmon. *Latin America. A Bibliography of Paperback Books.* Hispanic Foundation. Library of Congress. Washington, 1964. Also, see Charles J. Fleener and Ron L. Seckinger (eds.) *A Preliminary Guide to Latin American Paperback Literature.* Center for Latin American Studies. University of Florida. June, 1965.

Doctoral dissertations which would not long ago have gone unread are now being made available through advanced photocopying techniques.

Of very great significance to the added stature of Latin American politics have been increased opportunities for grants enabling professors and students to travel and to conduct research in the field. These are still far too few. It is still easier to create interest in Asia and Africa than in Latin America especially because of the enchantment with the "emerging" political systems in those areas.

All the large universities, nearly all the medium-large state universities, and many of the smaller universities and colleges of all types now have some emphasis on Latin American studies. Some of these offer advanced degrees specifically awarded for area study programs; most are no more than "emphases" within typical programs. A few universities have arranged contacts with Latin American universities for the establishment of programs abroad.

It is the purpose of this modest study to appraise the training in Latin American politics in the United States. It appears particularly appropriate to do so at this time because Latin Americanists are reaching that point in numbers and variety of output that a massive assault on Latin American politics may be possible in the next decade. Since the whole sweep of accomplishment so far is observable and encompassable, it may be useful to see what has been done, by whom, and to get some appreciation of the scope and depth of the work accomplished. Special attention will be given to Ph.D. programs; appraisal of newer trends will be explored. A brief survey of research problems will be made both as to peculiarly Latin American aspects, and as to comparative government broadly considered. Some suggestions then follow as to the more efficient handling of future research.

It is hoped that this survey will be of special interest to graduate students in Latin American politics who may want to scan the experience of Latin Americanists, of the variety *ciencia política*, who have worked in the initial phases of Latin American research.

RESEARCH OUTPUT ON
LATIN AMERICAN POLITICS

The significant research on Latin American politics in the universities of the United States is still encompassable. If all the books, articles, dissertations and other written efforts, excluding the massive histories of the colonial period and of the 19th century republics, were to be gathered together in an easily accessible collection, a reasonably diligent and able graduate student would be able to read all of them during the typical period of graduate study and research. This cannot be said of many deluged areas of political science and soon it will undoubtedly be impossible to say it of the Latin American area. It should be understood that reference here is made only to direct and reasonably integrated political studies, although one would include many works in anthropology, economics, geography, history, sociology, and literature. It is not easy to classify clearly and permanently what is "political" and one would in detailed research range widely, but a basic and complete survey of meaningful work in Latin American politics is still a manageable regimen for graduate study.

In the following pages there will be developed a chronological survey of Latin American political studies. This will be largely a quantitative survey although a number of the most significant names and works will be featured. It should be understood that the survey is limited in a number of ways: (1) works in the United States are the primary consideration, although a few works by foreign scholars are mentioned; (2) works are selected because they are clearly Latin American in content or deal with subjects that draw Latin America into a broad comparative framework, such as under the headings of "dictatorship" or "nation-building;" (3) to be considered are books and articles in selected journals in a number of closely associated disciplines; (4) "Latin America" refers only to the 20 independent systems usually associated with the term; and (5) "politics" is defined to exclude many studies on colonial matters, border controversies, other quite limited studies in international relations, and many general histories or reference works.

It should be appreciated that the selection of works in the United States is not intended to relegate to inferiority the works done elsewhere. The major burden of this study is to appraise the development of the study of Latin American politics in the higher educational institutions in the United States.

The scholarly output on Latin American politics has been nearly all contained within the approximately 60-year period from 1903. Although there were a few books of importance before 1903, the choice of that year as a starting point is motivated by the appearance of the earliest Ph.D. degrees granted specifically for research in Latin America. The whole 60-year period appears to suggest three convenient and justifiable parts: Before 1920, 1920-44 and 1945-64.

The Pioneering Years Before 1920

The development of much of the modern social science in the United States necessarily begins with a few history professors at the meccas of graduate work around the turn of the century. The geometric effect of these titans, followed through generations of succeeding historians and political scientists, is most impressive. At California, Harvard, Johns Hopkins, Pennsylvania, Wisconsin and Yale appeared most of the pioneers. A selected group of first-generation historians who strongly affected the Latin American studies would include Edward G. Bourne at Yale, Edward Channing at Harvard, John B. McMaster at Pennsylvania, Bernard Moses at California and Frederick J. Turner at Wisconsin and Harvard. Two of these — Bourne and Moses — wrote some of the earliest works in the Latin American field; the others launched students on careers in Latin American history from other bases of interest. Although he was not a professor, one cannot escape mentioning the eminent bookseller-historian, Hubert Bancroft, whose collection of materials founded the Bancroft Library at the University of California and who wrote voluminous histories covering a significant part of Latin America.

Although not as titanic in terms of authorship or the supervision of students, two political scientists who were contemporaries of the aforementioned historians and who left their mark significantly in diplomacy as well as teaching were Paul Reinsch who taught at Wisconsin from 1899 until 1913 and Leo S. Rowe who taught at Pennsylvania from 1895 to 1917 and who later became a much-beloved and effective figure in inter-American life as Director-General of the Pan-American Union. In addition, Reinsch and Rowe were presidents of the American Political Science Association in 1920 and 1921 respectively. Professors Reinsch and Rowe wrote significant articles on Latin American politics, among the earliest in the field appearing in the *American Political Science Review*.

Not technically a first-wave pioneer, but, in terms of great productivity and his long-range impact on Latin American studies undoubtedly a leading figure in the pioneer gallery, is Herbert Bolton. Bolton received a Ph.D. degree at Pennsylvania in 1899 and, although his research did not deal specifically with Latin America, he was exposed to the Latin American emphasis at that institution and he was probably influenced by McMaster in history and Rowe in politics. Later as a member of the history faculty at Texas (1901-1909) he began his studies in the history of the Spanish borderlands and through a long and splendid career at California of approximately thirty years, he launched over 100 students into Ph.D. degrees in Latin American history.[2] One of these was J. Lloyd Mecham who later, as a political scientist at Texas for decades, carved a considerable niche for himself in Latin

---

2 John Francis Bannon (ed.). *Bolton and the Spanish Borderlands*. Norman: University of Oklahoma Press, 1964. For Bolton's 54 Ph.D's up to 1930, see list in *New Spain and the Anglo-American West*, 2 vols., privately printed in Los Angeles in 1932.

American politics. Bolton students, a large and most enthusiastic fraternity, have left their mark across the whole face of Latin American history and politics in every part of the United States.

From 1903 to 1920 there sprang forward a new generation of Latin Americanists.[3]   There were 14 Ph.D's granted during the period which were clearly for research in Latin American topics: California produced 5, Yale 3, Harvard 3, Clark 1, Stanford 1 and Wisconsin 1. Among the recipients of these degrees were: William Spence Robertson (history, Yale), Hiram Bingham and Isaiah Bowman (geography, Yale; the former forever enshrined in Latin American annals for his discovery in 1911 of the Inca stronghold, Macchu Picchu, in the Peruvian Andes); three Bolton students at California (Charles Chapman, Herbert Priestley and Charles W. Hackett); and George W. Blakeslee (history, Harvard). Three of these were instrumental in turning out large numbers of students throughout the 1920's and 1930's: Robertson at Illinois, Hackett at Texas, and Blakeslee at Clark. Others who were granted degrees during this period and became important figures in the Latin American field, although not trained specifically in it as graduate students, were: Herman G. James and W. W. Pierson, at Columbia; Graham Stuart at Wisconsin; and Chester L. Jones who, after a Pennsylvania degree, taught at Wisconsin (numbering among his students Russell H. Fitzgibbon) and who also served as secretary-treasurer of the American Political Science Association from 1915 to 1918.

Nearly all of the publications during the period before 1920 were historical efforts, with a few geographical and economic works. The bridge to political science consisted primarily of two elements: the first was diplomatic history, oriented as it was largely toward international relations; and secondly, institutional and legalistic histories, especially of Spanish colonial institutions, and later, on constitutional ventures of 19th century Latin America. However, a few short articles appeared which pointed very clearly to much of what

---

3 Most of the information relating to Ph.D's before 1952 has been taken from Harry Kantor's *Unpublished Doctoral Dissertations and Masters' Theses Dealing with the Government, Politics and International Relations of Latin America*. Gainesville: University of Florida Press, 1953.

present political scientists consider to be their major thrusts. Paul Reinsch, Chester L. Jones and Leo S. Rowe wrote short pieces which we would regard today as not much more than public lectures on some of the characteristics of the Latin American political environment. However, these articles presented most of the channels along which much research has followed since: observations on awesome executive power, personalism, authoritarianism, constitutional dysfunction and socio-economic drawbacks to stability. Reinsch and Rowe had considerable opportunity to observe the operation of some Latin American systems and they presented two of the earliest single-country studies, of Chile and Argentina respectively.

By 1920 selected items of significance numbered 13 books and 10 articles. Among the books were the following: Bernard Moses, *Establishment of Spanish Rule in America* (1898); Edward G. Bourne, *Spain in America* (1918); and the beginning of a remarkable California series on Latin American colonial history by Donald E. Smith, Leslie B. Simpson and Charles Cunningham. Two works by non-Americans deserve special mention. In 1912 appeared James Bryce's *South America*, still regarded as a seminal work. Bryce wrote this during the time he served as British ambassador to the United States (1907-13); he also was president of the American Political Science Association in 1908. In 1913 appeared Francisco García Calderón's *Latin America* which has long served as a basic study of the Latin American political environment.

The ten articles referred to above are to be found in the *American Political Science Review*, the *Proceedings of the American Political Science Association* (the earlier form of the *APSR*), and in the *Annals* of the American Academy of Political and Social Sciences.

1920-44: (A Quarter-Century of Groundwork)

The ground-breaking quarter-century from 1920 through 1944 began auspiciously for Latin American studies with the election of two Latin Americanists to the presidency of the American Political Science Association: Paul Reinsch in 1920 and Leo S. Rowe in 1921. Leo S. Rowe's presidential address, published in the *APSR* in 1922, is still regarded as an excellent expression of the basic problems of

8

Latin American public affairs typified by the statement that Latin Americans need "to bring their social institutions into closer harmony with their political institutions." [4]

Graduate students appeared in greater numbers and those granted degrees in Latin American research began to appear steadily. In the institutions where the greatest activity occurred, the list of Ph.D's numbered 72 distributed as follows:

California	15	Texas	7	John Hopkins	3
Columbia	8	Chicago	6	Pennsylvania	3
Harvard	7	Duke	6	Wisconsin	3
Illinois	7	Clark	4	Yale	3

This list indicates a number of points worthy of mention. California shot into primacy as a graduate program, boosted tremendously by the geographic proximity of Latin American culture, the energies of Herbert Bolton and his colleagues, and the support of the materials supplied by the Bancroft Library. Texas built on the presence of Latin American culture and the early years of the Bolton career, followed by Bolton students, and gained early significance which it has maintained through the years. There are at least three other notable examples of virtuosity in the list: at Illinois, history students under William Spence Robertson; at Duke, history students under J. Fred Rippy (a Bolton student); and at Clark, history and international relations under George Blakeslee. Chicago, Columbia and Harvard sprang into Latin American studies from a position of general strength and prestige together with strong support from accessibility of research resources.

Among Ph.D's during this period, from all disciplines, who later had considerable impact on Latin American studies, one notes the following: Russell H. Fitzgibbon (Wisconsin), John Gillin (Harvard), Preston James (Clark), J. Lloyd Mecham (California), J. Fred Rippy (California), Charles Wagley (Columbia), A. C. Wilgus (Wisconsin) and Arthur P. Whitaker (Harvard). All of these scholars are still active, or recently retired, and represent anthropology, geo-

---

4 "The Development of Democracy on the American Continent," Vol. XVI, No. 1 (February, 1922).

graphy, history, political science and sociology. Fitzgibbon and Mecham are the political scientists of the group and both proved extremely productive in their careers at UCLA and Texas respectively. Indeed, by the end of the period, Fitzgibbon had already brought forward William S. Stokes who in turn was beginning to produce scholarly works.

In addition to the growing significance of political science from 1920 to 1945, and the continued contributions of history, the beginning of a Latin American interest in the ranks of sociology and social anthropology is noteworthy, especially at Chicago, Columbia and Harvard.

Approximately 60 important books may be selected out of the period. An appreciable percentage of these (about 40%) were published by university presses which had come into their own during the 1930s. At the following institutions, the presses were especially active in producing works in the Latin American field: California, Columbia, George Washington, Harvard, Minnesota and North Carolina. Most of the books published by university presses were, or were derived from, Ph.D. dissertations.

Among the notable publishing efforts sponsored by universities were two historical series. The California series, begun in the period before 1920, continued with Lillian Fisher's two books: *The Viceregal Administration in the Spanish Colonies* (1926) and *The Intendant System in Spanish America* (1929). The Inter-American Historical Series, published at North Carolina, under the general editorship of James A. Robertson, came forward in the 1930s with translated histories of seven Latin American countries: Argentina, translated by W. S. Robertson; Bolivia, by J. Lloyd Mecham; Brazil, by Percy A. Martin; Chile, by Isaac J. Cox; Colombia, by J. Fred Rippy; Mexico, by Charles W. Hackett and Peru, by W. W. Pierson. Each of these histories had originally been written by prominent Latin American historians.

The first books on the government of single Latin American political systems appeared in a series published by the Carnegie Institution: In 1921, Leo S. Rowe's *The Federal System of the Argentine Republic;* 1923, Herman G. James' *The Constitutional System of Brazil;* 1925, Graham Stuart's *The Gov-*

ernmental System of Peru; and in 1940, N.A.N. Cleven's *The Political Organization of Bolivia.* Although these works would by present standards appear thin, heavily legalistic and lacking in material on policy processes, they constituted important groundwork which, in fact, has not been completed even today for all 20 systems of Latin America.

Latin America was included in a number of broadly-based works of interest to comparative government. Under the editorship of Conyers Read, in 1938, appeared *The Constitution Reconsidered* with Latin American contributions by C. H. Haring, J. Lloyd Mecham and Percy A. Martin. Guy Stanton Ford's editorship of *Dictatorship in the Modern World,* in 1939, included a contribution by J. Fred Rippy.

Among other studies which became part of the basic library on Latin American politics were the following: Preston James' geographical *Latin America* (1942); George W. McBride, *The Land System of Mexico* (1923) and *Chile: Land and Society* (1936); J. Lloyd Mecham, *Church and State in Latin America* (1934); A. C. Wilgus as editor of *South American Dictators* (1937); William R. Crawford, *A Century of Latin American Thought* (1944); A. F. Macdonald, *Government of the Argentine Republic* (1942); Karl Loewenstein, *Brazil Under Vargas* (1942); Frank Tannenbaum, *The Mexican Agrarian Revolution* (1929) and *Peace by Revolution* (1933); John Gunther's *Inside Latin America* (1941); and a number of good histories and studies in international relations, including Mary Wilhemine Williams' *The People and Politics of Latin America,* the first edition of which appeared in 1930.

Proceeding to the matter of articles, the period from 1920 to 1945 was sparsely productive considering the span of time totalling twenty-five years. On a selected basis from those journals which were the major vehicles for articles on politics, there were perhaps 25 significant articles: 13 of these appeared in the *Hispanic American Historical Review* (which had started publication in 1918), 6 in the *American Political Science Review* and a scattering in other journals such as the *Annals* and *Inter-American Quarterly.* However, the content of the articles indicated a growing interest in some aspects of practical policy-making as well as continued interest in the purely institutional aspects. Articles continued to appear on such institutional aspects as federalism and constitutions but a number of probings into such practical matters as *caudillismo*, electoral processes, and the role of power centers such as the Church moved into the picture. Sociological and anthropological articles began appearing, especially in studies of Central American community structure, such as those accomplished by Sol Tax, Robert Redfield and Ralph Beals. This development was perhaps first heralded by the appearance of an article by Sol Tax in the *American Anthropologist* in 1939.

Sweeping over the whole period, 1920-44, one would conclude that political science had come into its own in the Latin American field but had not made more than ground-breaking impact into the real nature of politics and that only in a handful of systems. However, very portentous for the years to follow, some pioneering efforts had been made into some of the policy-making processes, particularly probing more deeply into the nature of Latin American leadership. All but a small number of Ph.D's in the Latin American field were still being trained in history. With Fitzgibbon at UCLA, A. F. Macdonald at California, Mecham at Texas, A. N. Christensen at Minnesota, Pierson at North Carolina, Graham Stuart at Stanford and William S. Stokes at Wisconsin, one found Latin Americanists operating from a base in political science. Others among political scientists could and did train Ph.D's in Latin American politics but they did so from another major interest within the discipline.

1945 to the Present: Preparing the Assault

When the spectacular achievements of our time are properly appreciated, not the least of these will be the awesome teaching and research output of the universities and colleges in the United States since the end of World War II. Although many are the grievances registered against this massive higher educational system, no one will ever be able to overlook the depth and breadth of its scholarly efforts. We have grown accustomed to using the physical sciences, especially mathematics and physics, as the indicator of this great academic adventure but, as anyone knows who has studied for a bachelor's degree in pre-World War II days, the richness and widely ranging research of the social sciences of our day are developments nearly as remarkable.

12

The factors contributing to the tremendous increase in student enrollments are well known and need no embellishment here. It is the author's hope that one day soon a substantial study will be made of the G. I. Bill which will serve to measure the far-reaching effects that legislation had on our national life. That enactment geared our educational system to the great assault to come later—as a result of prosperity and the deluge of "war babies." It sent college graduates into every corner of life in the United States; it trained large numbers of graduate students who have since helped to create an acceleration of knowledge touching every phase of human activity. The G. I. Bill also made an incalculable contribution to the transitional social and economic problems of the immediate postwar period. Its effect on graduate programs in Latin American studies can be clearly seen.

In the years 1945 through 1963 a steady and generally increasing stream of Ph.D's was turned out in the various disciplines that led to the training of Latin Americanists with political emphasis. For each year, with a total of 53 for 1961-63 averaged out at 18 each, the record is as follows:

1945 — 6	1951 — 21	1958 — 14
1946 — 5	1952 — 13	1959 — 26
1947 — 9	1953 — 18	1960 — 13
1948 — 8	1954 — 14	1961 — 18
1949 — 15	1955 — 20	1962 — 18
1950 — 14	1956 — 26	1963 — 18
	1957 — 9	

This list suggests four impulses with peaks at 1951, 1956, 1959, with possibly a fourth now in the making to climax in 1966 or 1967.

By 1951 the first group of postwar Latin Americanists had completed degrees including — to mention a few whose work in politics is evident in terms of published efforts: Robert Alexander, George Blanksten, Howard Cline, R.A. Gomez, John J. Johnson, Merle Kling, Wendell Schaeffer, Robert Scott, Kalman Silvert, Philip Taylor.

In the next six years through 1956 came the following: Marvin Alisky, S. Cole Blasier, Frank Brandenburg, Ben Burnett, David D. Burks, James Busey, Jesús Galíndez, William Glade, Harry Kantor, John J. Kennedy, Edwin Lieuwen, Leo Lott, Richard Morse, L. Vincent Padgett, Richard Patch, Frederick Pike, Karl Schmitt and Jordan Young.

Of the new crop since 1956, a significant number have already earned attention on the basis of publications: Charles Anderson, Daniel Goldrich, Richard Gray, Kenneth Johnson, John Martz, Frank Moreno, Martin Needler, Phyllis Peterson, John Plank, C. Neale Ronning, Ronald Schneider, and Peter Snow.

The output of books during the period since 1945 has increased markedly to the point that in 1963 alone at least 13 significant titles were published. The total output hovers around 100. Approximately half of these have been published by university presses with Columbia, Chicago, Harvard and Florida showing considerable activity. The great paperback boom which started during the middle 1950s has been a great boon to the Latin American field since class enrollments in Latin American courses have often not been substantial enough to warrant many hardback efforts. Without the university presses and the paperbacks, the Latin American field would still be only sparsely covered.

Writing efforts branched out in all directions, probing more deeply into every subject. One of the earlier publishing efforts of significance was Clarence H. Haring's excellent integration of the colonial period in *The Spanish Empire in America* (1947). The first textbook of primarily political orientation and covering all the republics in a country-by-country format appeared in 1949: A. F. Macdonald, *Latin American Politics and Government.* Other texts followed later with varying formats and scope: by Miguel Jorrin (1953), Pierson and Gil (1957), Harold E. Davis as editor of a collaborative effort (1958), William S. Stokes (1959), R. A. Gomez (1960), Martin Needler in a functional approach (1963) and as editor of a collaborative country-by-country approach (1964). Some Latin American systems appeared in broadly-based texts in foreign systems: Ogg and Zink's *Modern Foreign Governments* (1949) and Jordan Young's contributions on Mexico and Brazil in F. Morstein Marx's *Foreign Governments (1949).*

Significant books and collections of readings dealing with institutions and processes appeared: Harold E. Davis, *Makers of Democracy in Latin America* (1945) and *Latin American Leaders* (1949); Robert J. Alexander's prolific activity in such subjects as labor, Communism, the Bolivian revolution and political biography; John J. Johnson's *Political Change in Latin America* (1958), *Military and Society in Latin America* (1964) and *Continuity and Change in Latin America* (1964); Edwin Lieuwen's *Arms and*

14

Politics in Latin America (1960), *Generals Versus Presidents* (1964); R. N. Adams et al. *Social Change in Latin America Today* (1960) and K. H. Silvert's *Reaction and Revolution* (1961).

So well established had Latin America become in the paperback world that a special series has been undertaken by Alfred A. Knopf, Borzoi Books on Latin America, under the general editorship of Lewis Hanke, which includes: Frederick B. Pike, editor of *The Conflict Between Church and State in Latin America* (1964).

Studies of individual systems appeared in considerable number, some updating older efforts and others representing new efforts:

ARGENTINA

Ysabel F. Rennie. *The Argentine Republic*. 1945.
Carl C. Taylor. *Rural Life in Argentina*. 1948.
Robert J. Alexander. *The Peron Era*. 1951.
George I. Blanksten. *Peron's Argentina*. 1953.
John J. Kennedy. *Catholicism, Nationalism and Democracy in Argentina*. 1958.
T. F. McGann, translator of Jose L. Romero.
    A History of Argentine Political Thought. 1963.
James R. Scobie. *Argentina*. 1964.

BOLIVIA

Olen E. Leonard. *Bolivia*. 1952.
Robert J. Alexander. *The Bolivian National Revolution*. 1958.
C. W. Arnade. *Emergence of the Republic of Bolivia*. 1957.

BRAZIL

T. Lynn Smith. *Brazil*. 1946.
Preston James. *Brazil*. 1946. (geography)
L. F. Hill (ed.). *Brazil*. 1947.
Marvin Harris. *Town and Country in Brazil*. 1956.
Richard M. Morse. *Saõ Paulo*. 1958.
Charles Wagley. *An Introduction to Brazil*. 1963.

COLOMBIA

William M. Gibson. *The Constitutions of Colombia*. 1948.
K. Fluharty. *Dance of the Millions*. 1957.
John D. Martz. *Colombia*. 1961.

CENTRAL AMERICA

William S. Stokes. *Honduras.* 1950.
Sol Tax. *Heritage of Conquest.* 1952.
K. H. Silvert. *Guatemala* (2 vols.). 1954 and 1956.
Harry Kantor. *The Costa Rican Election of 1953.* 1958.
Ronald M. Schneider. *Communism in Guatemala,*
1944-54. 1958.
John D. Martz. *Central America.* 1959.
James L. Busey. *Notes on Costa Rican Democracy.* 1962.

CUBA

Lowry Nelson. *Rural Cuba.* 1950.
(And considerable publication on the Cuban Revolution
since 1960).

DOMINICAN REPUBLIC

Jesús de Galíndez. *La Era de Trujillo.* 1956.

ECUADOR

George I. Blanksten. *Ecuador: Constitutions and*
Caudillos. 1951.

MEXICO

Nathan Whetten. *Rural Mexico.* 1948.
Frank Tannenbaum. *Mexico.* 1950.
S. A. Mosk. *The Industrial Revolution in Mexico.* 1950.
Oscar Lewis. *Life in a Mexican Village.* 1951.
P. Romanell. *The Making of the Mexican Mind.* 1952.
H. F. Cline. *The U.S. and Mexico.* 1953.
William Tucker. *Mexican Government Today.* 1957.
Robert E. Scott. *Mexican Government in Transition.* 1959.
Clarence Senior. *Land Reform and Democracy.* 1960.
Merle Kling. *A Mexican Interest Group in Action.* 1961.
William Morton. *Woman Suffrage in Mexico.* 1963.
H. F. Cline. *Mexico: Revolution to Evolution 1940-60.*
1963.
Frank Brandenburg. *The Making of Modern Mexico.* 1964.

PERU

Harry Kantor. *Ideology and Program of the Peruvian*
Aprista Movement. 1953.
T. R. Ford. *Man and Land in Peru.* 1954.

Russell H. Fitzgibbon. *Uruguay*. 1954.
Philip B. Taylor. *Government and Politics of
Uruguay*. 1960.
Milton I. Vanger. *José Battle Ordoñez of Uruguay*. 1963.

VENEZUELA

Edwin Lieuwen. *Petroleum in Venezuela*. 1954.
―――. *Venezuela*. 1961.

During the period since 1945 it can be noted that all Latin American political systems have been described with the exception of Chile, Haiti and Paraguay (and these received some treatment in the form of professional articles).

A number of supplementary publishing ventures became invaluable aids. In 1948 the *Hispanic American Report* began a monthly country-by-country report under the editorship of Ronald Hilton at Stanford, supplying material in a conveniently chronological form until its last number in November, 1964. The American Universities Field Staff provided a large number of on-the-scene reports by well-selected correspondents. Quite recently, the Institute for the Comparative Study of Political Systems, under the direction of George Demetriou, Latin Americanist from Minnesota, has been publishing short pieces on the electoral process with material available so far on Argentina, Brazil, Chile, Peru and Venezuela, including analyses on recent elections by political scientists James Rowe, Martin Needler, Federico Gil and Charles Parrish. The Center of Latin American Studies at UCLA has for about ten years been publishing an annual *Statistical Abstract of Latin America,* a very usable compilation of social, economic and demographic tables for classroom use. Short studies by other institutes—North Carolina and Texas for example—have increased in number.

Probably the most dramatic development in books involving Latin America has taken place in very recent years with the advent of broadly comparative works into which Latin America in general or selected Latin American political systems have been drawn. As will be discussed in later pages, this has come about as a result of thorough self-appraisal among comparative governmentalists as to the state of the comparative approach to politics. Latin Ameri-

17

canists have been very prominent in this development, especially George I. Blanksten (Northwestern), Merle Kling (Washington, St. Louis) and Robert E. Scott (Illinois). Thus, in Almond and Coleman's *Politics of the Developing Areas* (1960), considered to be a most important milestone in comparative government, the Latin American contribution was made by Blanksten. The summing-up done by Coleman includes interesting comparative information on Latin American systems vis-a-vis other developing countries in Africa, Asia and the Middle East. In the same year, 1960, Seymour Lipset's *Political Man* included some Latin American data. In Karl Deutsch's *Nation-Building* (1963), Robert E. Scott contributed a Latin American example. However, it should be noted that Latin American contributions were absent from other significant comparative works such as Henry W. Ehrmann's *Interest Groups on Four Continents* and Sigmund Neumann's *Modern Political Parties.* In the Princeton series on political development Latin America is only incidentally handled. Unpublished papers motivated by conferences sponsored by the Comparative Politics Committee of the Social Science Research Council have dealt with Latin America, although they have circulated only in a small professional circle.

In 1963 appeared two other works of significance as broadly gauged comparative pieces: Almond and Verba's *Civic Culture* which includes Mexico in a survey of modern democratic variations; and Banks and Textor's *Cross-Polity Survey* which consists for the most part of a very lengthy computer print-out of data involving 115 political systems, the data presented in various combinations of variables. In 1964 came the *World Handbook of Political and Social Indicators* (Russett, Alker, Deutsch, Lasswell) wherein, as in the *Cross-Polity*, data on Latin American systems are included.

Turning to the output of articles in professional journals for the period since 1945, one discovers about 150 articles of importance, selected from the journals usually consulted for politics. During this period there were added a number of journals to serve as outlets for scholarly work and, unlike the preceding period which presented articles largely in two journals (*Hispanic American Historical Review* and *American Political Science Review*), there were by 1964 at least 20 journals which were publishing such articles, including journals in sociology, anthropology, economics, foreign affairs, public opinion, administration and law. A new journal appeared in 1959 which has proven to be a specialized producer: the *Journal of Inter-American Studies.*

The output of significant articles since 1945 is over 70% of the entire output since 1906, an indication of the acceleration of scholarly effort being experienced at this time. The numbers per year follow:

1945 —	9	1952 —	11	1959 —	14
1946 —	0	1953 —	5	1960 —	8
1947 —	4	1954 —	3	1961 —	12
1948 —	3	1955 —	6	1962 —	5
1949 —	12	1956 —	8	1963 —	11
1950 —	9	1957 —	5	1964 —	10
1951 —	12	1958 —	3	Total —	150

The bulk of these were published in the following journals:

American Political Science Review	36	(in 20 years)
Journal of Inter-American Studies	22	(in 6 years)
Western Political Quarterly	19	(in 16 years)
Hispanic American Historical Review	17	(in 20 years)
Journal of Politics	14	(in 16 years)
Inter-American Economic Affairs	14	(in 18 years)
Total	122	

Thus, 80% of the total output was in the 6 journals listed. The *American Political Science Review* and the *Hispanic American Historical Review* were the only journals in existence throughout the whole period of 20 years.

Some notable developments in professional articles might now be observed. Speaking very broadly, one notes two major trends. Along with the continuation of interest from the previous period in constitutions, executive power and basic institutions, the period from 1945 through 1951 featured an intense preoccupation with democracy and dictatorship; from 1952 through the remainder of the period came the beginning of deeper interest in the political processes with articles on parties and groups appearing in considerable number.

The postwar period was launched by a 6-man symposium appearing in June, 1945, in the *American Political Science Review*, under the editorship of Russell H. Fitzgibbon. Besides Fitzgibbon, participants were: Graham Stuart, Charles G. Fenwick, Arthur

Whitaker, William S. Stokes and Henry Reining, Jr. Stokes' contribution was "Parliamentary Government in Latin America" which has since been widely cited and used as the principal article on the subject. In 1950 came another symposium, in the March 1950 issue of the *APSR*, under the editorship of W. W. Pierson: in this effort Fitzgibbon as political scientist, Whitaker as historian, Sanford Mosk as economist and W. G. Crawford as sociologist tackled the "Pathology of Democracy in Latin America."

In 1951 appeared the first of a series of three articles, authored by Russell H. Fitzgibbon, on the appraisal and measurement of degree of democracy among Latin American systems. Professor Fitzgibbon was joined by Kenneth F. Johnson on the last of these. Together they comprise one of the few significant attempts to employ an opinion survey technique (polling Latin Americanists in the United States) followed by orderly tabulation and some statistical analysis. These articles provide a format for analysis of political change and represent a foundation for the refinement of this approach. The citations on these articles are:

Russell H. Fitzgibbon:
"Measurement of Latin American Political Phenomena:
A Statistical Experiment," *APSR*, XLV/2 (June, 1951).
"A Statistical Evaluation of Latin American Democracy,"
Western Political Quarterly, IX/3 (September, 1956).
Russell H. Fitzgibbon and Kenneth F. Johnson:
"Measurement of Latin American Political Change,"
APSR, LV/3 (September, 1961).

There is in the process another in this series, scheduled to appear in 1967.

As anyone knows, if he has delved into the methodological problems and interdisciplinary character of political studies, the impact of the sociologist was seen increasingly in the late 1940s and early 1950s. At first, in the Latin American field, this influence was evident in community studies principally in Mexico and Central America. Later, political sociologists began excursions into studies of community attitudes. In 1951 and 1952 the team of John Biesanz and Luke M. Smith published three articles of significance on Panamanian politics and political environment, these articles appearing in the *American Sociological Review,* the *American Journal of Sociology* and the *Journal of Politics.* Others in political sociology or social anthropology have been R. N. Adams, Ralph Beals, John Gillin, Seymour Lipset, Sol Tax, Charles Wagley and Nathan Whetten.

During the first half of the postwar period there were a number of articles of basic significance that were very widely cited and used in courses in politics: Ralph Beals on social stratification, Federico Gil on responsible parties, Harry Kantor on the Aprista movement, Merle Kling on a theory of power and political instability, Richard Morse on a theory of Spanish American government, William Stokes on violence as a power factor and Phillip Taylor on Uruguayan parties.

Looking at the whole period from a topical point of view, one observes a flurry of articles on parties, the military, the Church and students. Among those contributing strongly to political parties were: Charles W. Anderson, S. Cole Blasier, Russell Fitzgibbon, L. V. Padgett, Harry Kantor, Federico Gil, Philip Taylor, Frederick Pike, Leo Lott, R. A. Potash, Peter Snow. In 1964, John D. Martz surveyed the whole matter of the study of Latin American political parties. Articles on the military were contributed by: Olive Holmes, John J. Johnson, Theodore Wyckoff, L. N. McAlister, E. Lieuwen, R. Potash and Charles W. Anderson. The Church came under the scrutiny of L. E. Schuck and Frederick Pike, among others. Students were investigated by Biesanz and Smith, Frank Bonilla and Daniel Goldrich.

As a natural result of the involvements relating to the Cold War a number of scholars dealt with Communism in Latin American systems: S. Cole Blasier, Frederick Pike, Philip Taylor and Karl Schmitt.

Other articles on varying topics of special interest were written by Leo Lott on the Venezuelan executive, A. O. Spain on Mexican federalism, Frank Brandenburg on organized labor in Mexico, James Busey on contrasts between Costa Rica and Nicaragua, J. Lloyd Mecham on constitutions, Harold E. Davis on social thought, R. A. Gomez on executives, Charles W. Anderson on political development, Richard Morse on cities and urbanization, Jordan Young on Brazilian politics, and R.N. Adams on politics and anthropology in Spanish America.

An indicator of the future appeared in 1964 by Kenneth F. Johnson on causation and political instability which represents a confluence of methodology found earlier in Deutsch, Fitzgibbon, Kling and Lipset. It is an excellent example of the quantitative and statistical approach applied to some basic explorations in theory.

General Observations on the Output of 60 Years

The preceding paragraphs indicate the significant authorship and topical sweep of scholarly output on Latin American politics produced in the United States. If we stand back now and observe the effect of this effort, one is led to a number of conclusions.

There are a number of encouraging aspects. Outlets for publication have increased substantially. Studies on political dynamics and policy making are increasing in number. The bridging-over of sociology and anthropology to politics is showing promise. A few truly comparative works have appeared which promise extensions and elaborations in the future; in addition, new and promising frameworks for comparative exploration have been employed, especially in the cross-cultural orientation.

Still a matter of discouragement, however, are some alarming voids which present trends may fail to fill. At the risk of being labeled "old fashioned," detailed institutional descriptions of single Latin American political systems are still much needed in order to broaden the foundation for more sophisticated comparative studies. With travel grants favoring the more exciting frontier trends, it is increasingly difficult to finance simple institutional studies. Some areas suffering especially from this neglect are: political thought, public administration, local government and the judicial and legislative processes.

PH.D. PROGRAMS AND LATIN AMERICAN POLITICS

This survey of scholarly work in Latin American politics thus far has embraced research and writing in many areas besides political science, especially in history and sociology. The affinity of history and sociology for political science is acknowledged, and it is a mark of recent scholarly effort in politics that the disciplinary continuum of social anthropology-sociology-political sociology-political science often admits of only blurred dividing lines. This is especially true in the Latin American area specialty where the activity of sociologists and anthropologists, attracted by the bi-cultural nature of most of the area, moved into studies of community structure and attitudes.

Concentrating now on political science and its Ph. D. programs involving Latin American emphasis, a number of questions arise. How many Ph.D's? Where trained? What kinds of programs? Efforts to answer these questions occupy the following pages. However, the concentration in this study on the Ph.D. degree should not disparage many worthy projects which have led only to the M.A. degree. The M.A. degrees have been so numerous as to make accounting difficult.

Furthermore, nearly all significant M.A. efforts have probably either been published in some form or have become parts of subsequent Ph.D. dissertations.

With respect to holders of the Ph.D. degree, there is some difficulty in amassing the data required. As a starting point, there is Harry Kantor's *Unpublished Doctoral Dissertations and Masters Theses Dealing with the Government, Politics and International Relations of Latin America* (Gainesville, 1953); to bring this up-to-date, one may consult two recent publications: F.E. Kidder and

A. D. Bushong's *Theses on Pan American Topics* (Pan American Union, Washington, 1962) and F.E. Kidder's "Doctoral Dissertations in Latin American Studies, 1962-63," in *The Americas* (October, 1964). As an added check on these sources, the annual September issues of the *American Political Science Review* provide lists of recently completed dissertations (always subject to the reliability of political science departments in reporting data every year). Finally, the author's involvement with the personnel and bibliography in the field has supplied a name here and there. It is practically certain that a few names have been overlooked.

Since one of the interests of this survey was genealogical some attempts were made to discover the names of the supervising professors for all the dissertations thought to answer the standard of "political." A request for such information was sent to the reference librarians at those libraries housing the dissertations. To the great credit of those reference librarians, the author would most gratefully like to point out that every request was answered with the information supplied, which may well be some sort of record in the use of the questionnaire.

Ph.D. Dissertations on Latin American Politics

Although previous figures used (and relating to the whole stream of influence on Latin American politics as it developed in the United States), take us back 60 years, the dissertations which bear directly on politics, up through 1963, date back 41 years to 1923. These number 205 and were undertaken in 28 universities. The disciplines involved were: political science (113), history (76), literature (4), economics (5), law (3), sociology (2), geography (1) and education (1). As has been pointed out earlier, a number of people have moved into a Latin American specialty from training not directly with Latin American emphasis and therefore are not included in the above figures. In later pages, where we refer to some of these people and their bibliography, recognition will be accorded them.

The 113 Ph.D's that have completed dissertations, through 1963, on Latin American politics, *within political science*, were produced by 29 universities with the following breakdown:

24

California (Berkeley)	9	Princeton	5
Texas	9	American	4
California (L.A.)	8	Columbia	4
North Carolina	8	Pennsylvania	4
Harvard	7	Southern California	4
Stanford	7	Yale	4
Minnesota	6	Chicago	3
Wisconsin	6	Michigan	3
Georgetown	5		

Illinois, Kentucky, Notre Dame, Virginia, Washington (St. Louis) — 2 each
Duke, Florida, New York University, Northwestern, Ohio State, Pennsylvania State, Pittsburgh — 1 each

Scanning the list from a quantitative point of view, it is observable that the top four universities (California, North Carolina, Texas and UCLA) account for 30% of the total. All but a handful of the Ph.D's were produced in 17 universities. The Latin American specialty brings forward a few universities that have not found the highest favor in prestige-ranking schemes within political science as a whole: North Carolina and Texas are the most striking examples although Georgetown and Minnesota are notable.[5] On the other hand, some highly prestigious institutions seem to fall unreasonably below their marks in the production of Latin Americanists: Chicago and Michigan particularly, and, to a lesser extent, Columbia and Yale.

The impact of a single prominent specialist is clear in a number of instances. All of the 8 UCLA Ph.D's are the result of the supervision of Russell H. Fitzgibbon; J. Lloyd Mecham at Texas produced 7; Graham Stuart, 5 at Stanford; Federico Gil, 3 at North Carolina (and 3 other co-supervision efforts); Austin F. Macdonald, 3 at Berkeley; William S. Stokes, 3 at Wisconsin. In some institu-

---

5 In Albert Somit and Joseph Tanenhaus, "Trends in American Political Science: Some Analytical Notes," *American Political Science Review*, Vol. LVII, No. 4 (December, 1963), p. 936, one may see the 1925 Hughes Survey, the 1957 Keniston Survey as well as the 1963 Somit-Tanenhaus Survey on "prestige political science departments."

tions, Ph.D's in Latin American politics have come from highly scattered efforts, from other bases in political science besides the Latin American specialist: at Harvard, for example, supervisors have included Samuel H. Beer, Rupert Emerson (2), Carl Freidrich, Franklin Ford and Stanley Hoffman.

The Training Core for Ph.D's

Although 113 Ph.D's have received degrees based on work directly associated with some aspect of Latin American politics, probably only about half of these are now actively training students. Some have retired, a few are deceased, some have gone into university administration and a significant number have gone into some branch of the national government.

The 1961 Directory of the American Political Science Association lists 76 people who have indicated a primary interest in Latin America. This listing includes an appreciable number of graduate students and others not then in teaching; on the other hand, a significant number of people do not appear on the list. It would be most difficult to specify precisely the number of Ph.D's presently active in a teaching capacity. Probably the number of these who are actively engaged in the training of future Ph.D's is not much greater than 45, if one takes as criteria the matter of publication and/or location at institutions granting Ph.D's. One is tempted to put the figure closer to 30 people who operate at some 25 institutions, where the output of Ph.D's appears promising. (See Appendix I.)

The Fitzgibbon "Family"

Although it is perhaps not proper to describe the development of scholars by analogy to "family," it is nevertheless tempting to refer to the remarkable academic fecundity of Latin Americanists traceable to Russell H. Fitzgibbon during his years at UCLA (he has recently transferred to the Santa Barbara campus). The Fitzgibbon family is close to producing "great-grandchildren" and numbers 14 scholars in all. It is clearly in a class by itself when one considers total output of scholarly works. Including Fitzgibbon himself, at least 8 major books and 30 major articles can be attributed to this clan, not to mention minor efforts and unpublished works. The impact of this total effort has been sufficiently concentrated in time to constitute an effort largely undertaken in the last 15 years. Every member of the group has at least one published effort. Some have made deep and significant impressions. Besides Fitzgibbon, the works of William S. Stokes, George I. Blanksten, Harry Kantor, Ben G. Burnett, Robert E. Scott, Leo B. Lott, and L. Vincent Padgett are widely cited. At least 7 of the group are active in institutions where Ph.D. programs are in existence. The Stokes branch has itself produced 3 Ph.D's and the Blanksten branch at least 1. Blanksten and Scott have participated in the vanguard of Latin American politics with respect to national appraisals of the field and with respect to Latin American representation in the newly invigorated comparative government and its development.

New Activity

Judging by the reports in the *American Political Science Review*, in the September issues which report dissertations in progress, taken for the five years 1959 through 1963, there is new activity at varying levels of intensity and quantity. Vigorous activity is found at: Fletcher School of Law and Diplomacy, which reported 7 dissertations underway; Columbia with 5; North Carolina and Virginia, 4 each. Virginia is a newcomer to the productive ranks of Latin American politics and in good measure this is probably explained by the presence of John J. Kennedy (who has recently moved to Notre Dame). Significantly, California (Berkeley), Texas and UCLA do not report activity up to their standing in total output through the years, to some extent explained by the departure of Austin F. Macdonald (deceased), J. Lloyd Mecham (retired) and Russell H. Fitzgibbon (transferred to Santa Barbara campus), respectively.

Medium intensity appears at American and Harvard, with 3 reported dissertations each. At lesser degrees of intensity one finds Arizona, California (L.A.), Claremont, Duke, Florida, Georgetown, Illinois, Johns Hopkins, Maryland, Michigan, NYU, Northwestern, Pittsburgh, Princeton, Syracuse, Vanderbilt, Washington (St. Louis), Washington (Seattle), and Wisconsin.

Some institutions are not reported that will undoubtedly stir soon because of personnel additions, e.g., Iowa, Oregon, and Notre

Dame (Peter Snow, Daniel Goldrich and John J. Kennedy, respectively).

In replacing men who have departed for various reasons, experience appears to indicate that approximately 5 years will lapse before another Ph.D. may be expected. The same may be said of those institutions who are just beginning with Ph.D. programs. With respect to the former situation, institutions expecting such a change should perhaps provide a transitional arrangement to prevent lapses in output. Taking on a second man a few years in advance of such eventuality proves helpful. It is noted that North Carolina has maintained a fairly brisk output by overlapping the careers of W.W. Pierson and Federico Gil.

Ph.D. Programs

A survey of the matter of courses, requirements and the like presents too much variety to support much generalization. But in order to get some feeling for the matter, a rapid survey of university catalogues turned up a number of patterns. Catalogues change frequently, of course, and one would not want to cite chapter and verse blithely. Approximately 100 catalogues were surveyed; these represented nearly all the larger universities with outstanding facilities for graduate work, the state universities of all sizes and a number of smaller institutions where one might expect some attention to Latin America. Attention was paid only to Latin American courses under the discipline of political science or to closely associated programs, such as International Studies.

Most of the catalogues consulted (close to two-thirds of them) show only one or two Latin American politics courses; if two, a typical arrangement was a one-semester course in politics (either topically or country-by-country) and a course in the international relations category. In a significant number of cases, the politics course was an alternating one, given every other year.

Less than 20% of the institutions presented what would be considered emphasis on Latin American politics — at least three undergraduate courses and graduate courses and one graduate seminar. The following institutions commanded attention in that respect:

American, Arizona, Colorado, Columbia, California (L.A.), California (Santa Barbara), Florida, George Washington, Georgetown, Johns Hopkins, Minnesota, North Carolina, Southern California, Stanford, Texas, Tulane, Washington (St. Louis), Wisconsin.

This list does not include the institutions that could construct programs from such other vantage points as political parties, developing countries and political theory. This would explain the omission from the list of California (Berkeley), Cornell, Harvard, Illinois, Indiana, Michigan, Ohio State, Princeton, Syracuse, Washington (Seattle), Vanderbilt and Yale. Each of these has some emphasis on Latin America and each has turned out Ph.D's who are considered Latin Americanists with politics training but their courses in Latin American politics are few or even non-existent at present. Some institutions have special organizational slants worthy of mention such as the Fletcher School of Law and Diplomacy which has excellent courses touching on Latin American diplomacy or economics; Massachusetts Institute of Technology has a strong program in international studies which features Latin American material.

The broadest bases in political science of Latin American orientation, in terms of specific courses offered, are to be found at American, Florida, North Carolina and Texas. These institutions offer not only full-year courses in politics of Latin American political systems, international relations or inter-American relations, and accompanying seminars, but also additional courses such as political theory or policy problems. In addition, they have strong Latin American emphases in other departments.

Latin American Studies

A large number of U.S. colleges and universities list programs which typically are called Latin American Studies although a few use the term Hispanic-American Studies or, fewer still, Ibero-American Studies. Some emphasize Luso-Brazilian or perhaps simply Brazilian Studies. One can determine what these mean in terms of graduate training only by careful scrutiny of each program. Typically the use of the term Latin American Studies means simply an "emphasis" or "concentration" with the undergraduate majors

29

and the graduate degrees taken in one of the traditional departments. The following variations exist:

1. Simply a committee or council charged with the building up of library materials or the advising of students who want a Latin American emphasis.
2. An integrated program of undergraduate courses specifically laid out in such a way a student may have a heavy concentration in Latin America but the major is in one of the traditional disciplines.
3. A program of area study in which one may major or minor for an undergraduate degree.
4. A program of area study which leads to graduate degrees or perhaps certification; some go to the M.A. only; some do not allow Ph.D. but accept a minor in in area study with a major in one of the traditional disciplines.

The question of "area study" as against training in one of the traditional disciplines has long been a matter of dispute among Latin Americanists. The author has heard the debate a number of times and recalls especially a panel on the matter held in Denver in the fall of 1959 on the occasion of the 7th Annual Conference of the U.S. National Commission for UNESCO, during which Ronald Hilton of Stanford upheld the "area study" side and a number of others, notably historian Lewis Hanke (then at Texas, now at Columbia) upheld the "departmental" side. The verdict so far is still clearly in favor of the traditional departmental approach, the main support for the argument being the demand for teachers with strongly disciplined training who are going to be employed by the traditional departments where they will usually have to teach something besides Latin America. At the center of such a debate is much involvement with the nature of "discipline" and the degree to which "specialization" should govern curricula.

Ronald Hilton's zeal for the area study approach to graduate study at Stanford, which centered on a training program featuring the publication of *Hispanic American Report*, led to some academic disturbance at Stanford in which the traditional departmental approach triumphed late in 1964. The upshot was a rearrangement with respect to graduate work in favor of the departments and led also, one hopes only temporarily, to the cessation of publication of the *Hispanic American Report,* a monthly report of considerable assistance to all Latin Americanists.

Some of the more broadly based Latin American Studies programs are organized into Institutes or Centers as at American, Columbia, Florida, NYU (Brazilian Institute), North Carolina, Texas, Tulane (Middle American Institute) and U.C.L.A. Publications are put forward under the imprint of these institutes and many important aids made available. For example, U.C.L.A. publishes annually the *Statistical Abstract of Latin America* and a large number of studies and bibliographic works have come out of Florida.

A number of institutions have been granted substantial sums from various foundations for their Latin American programs. In 1947 a certain recognition of specialties dividing the Latin American area was advanced when the Carnegie Foundation awarded funds to North Carolina for Spanish South America, to Texas for Mexico, to Tulane for Middle America and to Vanderbilt for Brazil. The Kellogg Foundation more recently granted a large sum to the Johns Hopkins School for Advanced International Affairs in order to establish Latin American emphasis. The Ford Foundation, through its Foreign Area Fellowship Training program, has assisted a number of institutions. Through a contract with the Agency for International Development, the Land Tenure Center at the University of Wisconsin has developed a program in special aspects of Latin American research.

National Coordination

The whole burgeoning field of Latin American studies is rapidly reaching the point where some national coordination appears necessary. There are a number of regional councils for Latin American studies which so far serve only to bring professors together to exchange information by the usual format of panels, papers and discussions. The Hispanic Foundation of the Library of Congress has gathered information for a Directory of Latin Americanists. The Latin American Studies Committee of the Social Sciences Research Council has performed an important function, largely as a medium through which research orientation has trickled down to the grass roots. But there has been some difficulty forming a lasting national organization with ability to give a sweeping view to studies being undertaken and to organize some division of scholarly effort. In 1960 an effort was made in the establishment of the Association for Latin American Studies which began with the publication of a *Quarterly Bulletin* but apparently did not provide the spark.

A more encouraging start has recently been made in the creation of the Latin American Research Review Board which came out with the *Latin American Research Review*, Fall 1965. The member institutions are: Arizona, California (Berkeley), California (L.A.), Columbia, Cornell, Florida, Illinois, Indiana, Kansas, Louisiana State, Michigan State, New Mexico, NYU, North Carolina, Notre Dame, Ohio State, Oregon, Penn State, Pennsylvania, Pittsburgh, Puerto Rico, Stanford, Texas Tech, Texas, Tulane, Washington (St. Louis), Wisconsin, Yale, and the Hispanic Foundation.

In the first number appears a partial round-up of research in progress as well as articles on special research adventures in social stratification, urbanization and land reform. It is hoped that this publication will serve as a clearing-house for Latin Americanists.

PROBLEMS AND TRENDS

Naturally the study of Latin American politics is subject to whatever problems assail political science in general. This is not a proper place to trot out all the alleged drawbacks of a political science. The question as to whether political science is a science or not or the matter of how best to stretch toward general theories of politics or how to gain a high degree of predictability will always haunt us, or at least through the foreseeable future. This modest survey is aimed at humbler goals.

The chief difficulty for Latin Americanists in political science is encountered somewhat short of the ultimate targets for political science. We must first overcome the massive problems of gathering information in depth. Latin Americanists have carved out a great piece of the earth's political systems which, if covered as an area, necessarily is treated very superficially. Since we must treat the whole area, or a substantial part of it, in the classroom, we cannot look for great profundity in the typical range and scope of our courses. We can hope that a typical professor's research inclinations have taken him into sufficient depth somewhere in this massiveness and that means can be found to organize the whole effort sufficiently.

Problems of Method

If we can perhaps omit any involvement herein with the methodological problems of political science in general, we should however engage to some extent the matter of comparative government as an approach within political science. Latin Americanists are almost all comparative governmentalists within the great mansion of political science. Anyone who has been interested of late in comparative government knows that there have occurred in the past ten years a considerable amount of soul-searching among comparative governmentalists and appraisal of the comparative approach as to its probabilities in reaching toward general theories, predictability or even meaningfully arranged knowledge. Some refer these days to the "new comparative government." Whether anything about it is new or not is debatable but clearly a new spirit and communicability have developed. In a recent article which presented the results of a survey among political scientists, comparative government was regarded as second only to "general politics and behavioralism" in terms of "significant work done" and, in terms of the ratio of favorable to unfavorable responses, it was rated first.[6]

The self-appraisal among comparative governmentalists was significantly expressed by 1953 when the Social Science Research Council, through its summer seminar on comparative politics, drew up a statement published in the *American Political Science Review* in September, 1953. This statement, together with elaborations in various journals, has served as a sort of charter for the "new comparative government." The result was wide communication of the kind of effort that would be necessary to wield the comparative approach more effectively: better understanding of the nature of comparability, useable classificatory schemes, the various levels of the comparative approach and the suitability of certain unifying terminology (much of which comes from sociology). A considerable scramble has ensued to make comparative government "truly comparative." A good deal of financial support has developed for these efforts and the shelf of literature resulting from this spurt is growing.

Among the Latin Americanists who have participated on the frontier of the "movement" during conferences under the sponsorship of the Social Science Research Council have been George I. Blanksten, Merle Kling and Robert E. Scott. Referring more broadly to political science in general, the efforts of Almond,

---

6 Albert Somit and Joseph Tanenhaus, "Trends in American Political Science: Some Analytical Notes," *American Political Science Review*, Vol. LVII, No. 4 (December, 1963), pp. 941-2.

Coleman, Deutsch, Lasswell and Sigmund Neumann, among others, have helped to draw Latin America into a broader comparative framework.

Latin Americanists, it may be said, have felt a certain smugness throughout this development. For it may well be true that among comparative governmentalists at large, Latin Americanists have been the least "parochial," to use the term that was thought especially damning. Latin Americanists have had to be comparative-minded. Although we may have belabored the Argentine constitution a bit too much, the classroom orientation and the hypothesizing of the Latin Americanists have been considerably comparative. This has taken place at several levels: with relation to Latin American systems interacting with each other; more broadly, with respect to North American or European institutions; and, conceptually, with respect to democracy, leadership and socio-economic factors. It may be that this was largely classroom-oriented and did not reach published form in any dramatic way but one can say, at the very least, that Latin Americanists had already served a long apprenticeship.

The earliest efforts of political scientists in the Latin American area were very mindful of one of the first great lessons of comparative government: recognition of the gap between theory and practice, constitutions and reality, the "ought to be" and "is." The Latin American area may have served indeed as the first great exposition of this most bedevilling aspect of political systems; the theory-practice gaps in the traditionally developed-in-depth systems, Britain and the United States, were much narrower and were not as pervasive and as frustrating to the understanding of those systems. Leo S. Rowe marked out this arena for scholarly struggle in his presidential address to the American Political Science Association in 1921 when he referred to the basic problem of Latin Americans: squaring their social efforts with their constitutions. Latin Americanists were also pioneers in the developing-country approach which is after all basically an elaboration of the very old thesis that socio-economic barriers affect stability and maturity.

If one were to choose the greatest contributions which Latin Americanists had made in advance of the recent impulse in comparative government, and which provided an existing base for the impulse, one might suggest two special elaborations of the theory-practice divergence: the nature of the Latin American executive power as compared with other types elsewhere and the study of various aspects of the democratic processes. There is evident in much research today a certain employment of Latin America as a possible indicator of the future of newly emerging systems.

But in speaking of these old orientations among Latin Americanists in political science one is compelled to admit that not much published scholarly effort has been produced in evidence and that there has been lacking broad and more meaningful use of hypotheses which were being tentatively voiced within the Latin American context.

Research Problems

The study of Latin American political systems has suffered from lack of financial support for research in the field. It is much easier to gain acceptance for a research design involving Africa, Asia or the Middle East. Grants for Latin American study have, however, increased in recent years through the large foundations and various government agencies. In the last few years about 60 scholars have received grants from funds administered jointly by the Social Sciences Research Council and the American Council of Learned Societies. From smaller foundations come those such as the Doheny fellowships which have been specifically for Latin American research (with a preference for Chile).

Even if the financial aspects were completely remedied, the nature of field research in Latin America offers other problems. This has been the subject of many a conference. At the broadest level, the matter has been explored with respect to the developing country, or the non-western countries, as in Kahin, Pauker and Pye, "Comparative Politics of Non-Western Countries" in the *American Political Science Review* (XLIX, 4: December, 1955). Under Robert E. Ward's editorship (with Frank Bonilla, James S. Coleman, Herbert H. Hyman, Lucian W. Pye and Myron Weiner) has appeared a synthesis of the matter: *Studying Politics Abroad* (Little, Brown; 1964), sponsored by the Committee on Comparative Politics of the Social Science Research Council. In this work can be found a round-up of the problems relating to the research environment, interviewing, and documentary research as well as valuable appendices on research materials and their locations.

The specific Latin American version of the research problems has also been much appraised. In addition to shorter observations such as Harold E. Davis' *Social Science Trends in Latin America* (Washington, 1950) and short reports in the Social Science Research Council's *Items*, there have been at least two recent and substantial explorations. Charles Wagley has edited *Social Science Research on Latin America* (Columbia University, 1964) which consists of a series of papers presented at a Stanford meeting in the summer of 1963 under the sponsorship of the Joint Committee on Latin American Studies (Social Science Research Council and American Council of Learned Societies). In this work, Merle Kling presents the special problems of political science. Another survey appears in the form of the September, 1964, issue of *The American Behavioral Scientist*, entitled "Social Research in Latin America," the contribution from political science again handled by Merle Kling in an article entitled "Area Studies and Comparative Politics."

The distillation of all of these might be presented in a few words. There is need for greater communication between social scientists in Latin America and their counterparts in the United States. Documents are difficult to find in usable form, or in unbroken series, and their reliability is questionable. The cultural environment interposes many difficulties and suggests caution in applying some of the bolder techniques used in the United States. But, capping it all, there is a need for well-designed research projects which would take one efficiently and promisingly into the policy-making processess. Kling lists 35 possible research projects in the Wagley book.

(It has been the author's experience that, except for some sociological studies, it is difficult to find any considerable assistance in the works of Latin American scholars.) In political science, there are very few studies that would be significant by North American standards. Most of the pieces are highly legalistic, turning on lengthy interpretations of constitutions or historical developments; or they may be European-style texts consisting largely of quotations from other authorities; or they are highly partisan affairs. Latin Americans, in many cases for perfectly understandable

37

reasons, show a great disinclination to comment too closely on policy-making in terms of "who gets what, when, how." If the approach is used, it is probably by disaffected and bitter politicians whose detachment from an emotional motivation is quite in doubt.

Trends

There are four major trends in the study of Latin American politics which call for comment.[7]

1. *There has been some attempt to establish basic theoretical positions relating to the Latin American political environment.* Two articles might be mentioned here: Richard M. Morse's "Toward a Theory of Spanish American Government" (1954), which set forward some suggestions relating to latent Machiavellianism and Merle Kling's "Towards a Theory of Power and Political Stability in Latin America" (1956) which suggested some relationships between socio-economic factors and instability. Others are in the making that will undoubtedly be published soon.

2. *An emphasis on the study of groups in policy-making* is increasingly evident. Studies of single political systems are now emphasizing such matters, a good example being Robert E. Scott's *Mexican Government in Transition.* Merle Kling's *A Mexican Interest Group in Action* is a shorter but pithy study directly on policy-making. A growing number of articles are appearing on the community power structures; a few case studies on decision-making are available. Broader in scope and an important classificatory approach to the whole subject was George I. Blanksten's "Political Groups in Latin America" (1959) which presented Latin American substance for the typology of interest articulations (associational, non-associational, institutional, anomic). A glance at recently designed research projects and doctoral dissertations suggests that we are shortly to hear from others on elaborations of these approaches.

Some admirable reports are available by the reporters of the American Universities Field Service which give invaluable on-the-spot observations of the political processes by trained social scien-

---

7 All the articles referred to in this section can be found in the bibliographical appendix with full citations.

tists. The reports of Richard Patch, Frank Bonilla, James Rowe, Kalman Silvert and others are excellent insights into the matters of interest to political scientists.

3. *The application of quantitative methods* is underway although not as yet with much material from field surveys. Russell Fitzgibbon's series of articles on Latin American democracy and political change which were published in 1951, 1956, and 1961, employed modern survey technique by which a number of Latin Americanists in the United States were asked to rate Latin American political systems with respect to a number of criteria; statistical evaluations of these were made; the factor of degree of knowledge of each contributor for each item was reckoned which attempted to correct findings accordingly. Collaborating with Fitzgibbon on the 1961 version was Kenneth F. Johnson who has carried his enthusiasm forward into a recent article, chiefly a display of the quantitative technique applied to a basic problem of political environment: "Causal Factors in Latin American Political Instability," *Western Political Quarterly* (XVII, 3; September, 1964).

4. Perhaps the most dramatic trend of recent years has been the *gathering of Latin American political systems and data into broader comparative frameworks.* From the middle 1950's on, very considerable attention has been paid to various classification schemes for cross-cultural consideration of political systems. The Almond classification scheme has been widely used, although increasingly considered to be unnecessarily simplified: a fourfold approach including anglo-american, continental european, totalitarian and pre-industrial political cultures. Also attracting attention has been the Shils classification: political democracy, tutelary democracy, modernizing democracy, totalitarian oligarchy, and traditional oligarchy; Almond and Coleman later added to this scheme: terminal colonial democracy and colonial or racial oligarchy. These schemes have had the effect of moving Latin American systems into broader comparative consideration. Also, under the heading of economic development have come schemes for classification bringing systems into some meaning comparatively with respect to maturity and modernity.

One of the earlier milestones of these developments was Almond and Coleman, *Politics of the Developing Areas* (1960).

In this work George I. Blanksten supplied the contribution on Latin America. The book focuses broadly across a political culture after assembling data on an areal basis. It brings together all the currents of the "new" comparative government. Almond wrote the framework of the design and in so doing accomplished a sweeping integration of the concepts and terminology of the recent trends in comparative government; contributors supplied information on their area specialties to fit the design; Coleman took the data and arranged them into some tabular expressions. The tables are especially interesting in that they array the political systems of Latin America, the Middle East, Africa and Asia with respect to their modernity and competitiveness and also relate these positions to certain socio-economic indices.

On a smaller scale have been a number of broad conceptual exercises, also of cross-cultural nature. Almond and Verba's *The Civic Culture* (1963) is a significant survey of political attitudes in Germany, Italy, Great Britain, Mexico and the United States. Its probings arouse considerable interest in aspects of that subtle balance of moderation and stability which is the civic culture. This approach is apparently being expanded in works presently underway. Seymour Lipset and Karl Deutsch have also explored socio-economic criteria cross-culturally from a conceptual base.

Comparative politics is being increasingly assisted by the use of electronic computers. The most massive evidence of this so far has been the Banks and Textor *Cross-Polity Survey* (1963). In this work, 115 political systems were coded with respect to 57 raw characteristics. Each of these was then applied to 194 dichotomous variables. Most of the book consists of a selected portion of the computer print-out resulting from that process, although there is an introduction setting forth the methodological approach and explanations of the coding procedure. The amount of data produced is staggering and perhaps only a beginning has been made to date toward analyzing the meaning and usefulness of this reservoir. (There is much material here for investigation via graduate papers and theses) The first point of analysis should be a thorough study of the basic coding since this involved a number of subjective decisions, such as coding political systems on such elusive matters as "type of ideological orientation," "representative character" and "leadership charisma."

40

Thus, Latin Americanists are being swept along by exciting and vast possibilities. It is probable that we shall see some ventures of comparative scope that will open new channels. Especially promising seem to be the channels that will broaden, by inclusion of the cross-cultural outlook, the basis on which we generalize about Latin America.

THE FUTURE

Latin Americanists who are of the persuasion *ciencia política* find themselves at a milestone in the development of their specialty. All the signs indicate that a massive assault may soon begin on all parts of Latin American politics. Methodologically, some exciting trends are noticeable. It seems to the author that it should be possible to harness all this energy more efficiently. There is, after all, a strong specialty-identity here, generations in the making. Much has already been done, through the efforts of special committees of the Social Science Research Council and other professional conferences, to enhance this identity. But with the increasing tempo of activity the problems of communication and the possibilities of duplicated efforts increase. Perhaps Latin Americanists can avoid these pitfalls that have already claimed many victims in some other areas within political science.

National Organization

The effort taken up a few years ago to create a lively Association for Latin American studies should be renewed. Such a clearinghouse will soon be indispensable. Not only the matter of simple communication is involved but also the need for machinery to coordinate scholarly effort is very pressing. It takes a considerable and extravagant amount of research time to acquaint one's self with the work being done, in order not to waste talent and facilities. It is quite possible to enlarge on the system of data storage and retrieval that now exists at the Inter-University Consortium for Political Research with headquarters at the University of Michigan.

The very recently organized Latin American Research Board through its first issue of *Latin American Research Review* (Fall, 1965) may possibly have provided the institution and the approach through which this may be done. In the Current Research Inventory section of the issue appears a topical index for uniform classification of research projects as well as a suggestion for the use of a McBee Keysort card system as a means of storing research information.

Research at Three Levels

At those universities offering Ph.D. degrees in Latin American politics (that is, political science with a Latin American emphasis), it would be well to contemplate research efforts at three levels. Every comparative governmentalist probably thinks in such tri-level terms, but their thoughts should be better organized for communication. Each institution should have its own *country-specialty*, the careful and persistent building in depth on the politics of at least one system, or perhaps one country for each Latin American specialist. The increasing hunger of computers for more data will increase the need for this degree of specialization. The most desirable situation will naturally be that in which the country-specialty will be adopted throughout all disciplines at such institutions, although it is appreciated that this is a most difficult interdisciplinary interest to create overnight. Perhaps in time the drift of academic talent will be channeled in some orderly fashion after the establishment of a tentative pattern. It might be mentioned that something of an effort of this sort has begun with respect to the acquiring of research materials under the leadership of the Farmington Plan Committee of the Association of Research Libraries. Universities are indicated as the possible repositories of the materials of certain countries and are then held responsible for reporting acquisitions to the Library of Congress Union Catalogue.

At the second level, each university sufficiently staffed with a Latin American specialty in political science should develop a *topical or conceptual specialty*, such as some facet of democracy, personalism or policy-making. Probably no one institution will be able to swallow the whole of any topic. The matter of coordination and communication will be critical at this level.

43

At the third level, and probably not to be considered a strong possibility at other than the best-staffed institutions in all disciplines, attempt should be made to establish programs for the *fusion of efforts to a cross-cultural design.* Some institutions will be able to fuse Latin America with the Middle East, others with Africa and so on.

The Undergraduate Courses

Finally, it would be well to remember the responsibility for the teaching of solid, up-to-date courses for the undergraduate. Let research and specialty work to the advantage of the undergraduate as well as the graduate student. As the massive assault increasingly engages us, we shall stand in some danger of carelessly proliferating courses in Latin American politics. In order to accomplish a first-rate program in political science, it is not necessary to teach everything but it is necessary to teach solidly and well in a few basic courses for the undergraduate.

In any future meetings on the state of Latin American politics it is hoped that the needs of undergraduates as well as graduate students will guide the establishment of some system for better coordination of scholarly effort.

LATIN AMERICANISTS TEACHING
IN POLITICAL SCIENCE

This list has perhaps been compiled with certain arbitrariness and therefore names are missing that would under another set of criteria be included. An attempt has been made to limit the list to those persons who (1) have earned Ph.D's up through early 1964, (2) are, or were recently, teaching at the college level, (3) have established some identity in political science even though trained in another discipline, and (4) have some publications to their credit or, if not, are located in positions that make equivalent demands. The very latest information on all these points is impossible to secure precisely.

By referring to the bibliography in Appendix II one can connect the names with research interests.

Name	Sources and Directors of Ph.D's.	Location
Alisky, Marvin H.	Texas, 1953; Sanchez, Mecham	Arizona State
Anderson, Charles W.	Wisconsin, 1960; Epstein	Wisconsin
Anderson, Robert W.	California, 1960; Bellquist	Puerto Rico
Baker, Richard D.	North Carolina, 1963; Gil	Oklahoma
Blanksten, George I.	UCLA, 1949; Fitzgibbon	Northwestern
Blasier, S. Cole	Columbia, 1954;	Pittsburgh
Brown, Lyle C.	Texas, 1964;	Baylor
Burnett, Ben G.	UCLA, 1955; Fitzgibbon	Whittier
Busey, James L.	Ohio State, 1952; Helms	Colorado
Cardenas, Leonard	Texas, 1964; Mecham	Texas Western
Cope, Orville G.	Claremont, 1963; Stokes	Wisconsin (Milwaukee)
Cornelius, William G.	Columbia, 1956;	Agnes Scott
Davis, Harold E.	Western Reserve, 1933; Cole	American
Dix, Robert H.	Harvard, 1962; Beer	Yale
Fitzgibbon, Russell H.	Wisconsin, 1933; Jones	California (Santa Barbara)
Francis, Michael J.	Virginia, 1963; Kennedy	Notre Dame
Gabbert, Jack B.	Texas, 1963; Mecham	Washington State
Gil, Federico	Habana, 1941;	North Carolina
Glick, Edward	Florida, 1955; Hartmann	Temple
Goldrich, Daniel	North Carolina, 1959; Gil	Oregon
Gomez, Rosendo A.	Minnesota, 1950; Christensen	Arizona
Goodspeed, Stephen S.	California, 1947; Harris	California (Santa Barbara)
Gould, Lyman J.	Michigan, 1958; Kallenbach	Vermont
Gray, Richard B.	Wisconsin, 1957; Stokes	Florida State

Name	Sources and Directors of Ph.D's.	Location
Harris, Louis K.	UCLA, 1956; Fitzgibbon	Kent State
Harrison, Horace V.	Texas, 1951; Hackett	Maryland
Hayton, Robert D.	California, 1954; Macdonald	Hunter
Heubel, Edward J.	Minnesota, 1955; Anderson	Michigan State (Oakland)
Houston, John A.	Michigan, 1951; Preuss	Knox
Johnson, Kenneth F.	UCLA, 1963; Fitzgibbon	Southern California
Kahle, Louis G.	Texas, 1951; Mecham	Missouri
Kantor, Harry	UCLA, 1952; Fitzgibbon	Florida
Kelso, Paul	Ohio State	Arizona
Kennedy, John J.	Columbia, 1954; Tannenbaum	Notre Dame
Kitchen, James D.	UCLA, 1955; Fitzgibbon	San Diego State
Kling, Merle	Washington U., 1949; Lien	Washington (St. Louis)
Lewis, Frank M.	Texas, 1955; Mecham	Toledo
Lott, Leo B.	Wisconsin, 1954; Stokes	Montana
Mack, Raymond D.	Texas	Texas Tech. College
Martz, John D. III	North Carolina, 1963; Gil	North Carolina
Mecham, J. Lloyd	California, 1923; Bolton	Texas (Retired)
Menez, Joseph F.	Notre Dame, 1953; Gurian	Loyola (Chicago)
Moreno, Frank J.	NYU, 1964;	NYU
Morton, Ward M.	Texas, 1941; Mecham	Southern Illinois
Moses, Carl C.	North Carolina, 1958; Pierson, Gil	Virginia Polytechnic Inst.
Neal, Joe W.	Texas, 1958; Mecham	Texas
Nealley, W. Grafton	Stanford, 1948; Stuart	Adelphi
Needler, Martin C.	Harvard, 1960; Ford	New Mexico
Padgett, L. Vincent	Northwestern, 1955; Blanksten	San Diego State
Parrish, Charles J.	North Carolina	Texas
Peterson, Phyllis J.	Michigan, 1962; Eldersveld	Indiana (Jefferson)
Plank, John N.	Harvard, 1959; Emerson	Brookings Inst.
Ronning, C. Neale	Minnesota, 1958; McLaughlin	Tulane
Schaeffer, Wendell G.	California, 1950; Macdonald	Pittsburgh
Schmitt, Karl M.	Pennsylvania, 1954; Whitaker	Texas
Schneider, Ronald M.	Princeton, 1958; Monro	Columbia
Scott, Donald H.	Southern California, 1959; Berkes	Long Beach State
Scott, Robert E.	Wisconsin, 1949; Stokes	Illinois
Silvert, Kalman H.	Pennsylvania, 1949; Kale	Dartmouth
Snow, Peter G.	Virginia, 1960; Kennedy	Iowa
Stokes, William S.	UCLA, 1943; Fitzgibbon	Claremont
Taylor, Philip B.	California, 1950; Macdonald	Johns Hopkins (Washington)
Tucker, William P.	Minnesota, 1945	Puerto Rico
Wells, Henry	Yale, 1947; Coker	Pennsylvania
Young, Jordan M.	Princeton, 1953; Monro	Pace

SELECTED BIBLIOGRAPHY

METHODOLOGY

Almond, Gabriel. "Introduction," in Almond and Coleman, *Politics of the Developing Areas*. Princeton, 1960.

Banks, Arthur S. and Robert B. Textor. *The Cross-Polity Survey*. M.I.T. Press, 1963.

Davis, Harold E. *Social Science Trends in Latin America*. American University Press, 1950.

Eckstein, Harry and David Apter. *Comparative Politics*. Free Press, 1963.

Kahin, G.M., G.J. Pauker and L.W. Pye. "Comparative Politics of Non-Western Countries," *American Political Science Review*, Vol. XLIX, No. 4 (December, 1955).

Macridis, Roy. *The Study of Comparative Government*. Random House, 1955.

Macridis, Roy and Bernard Brown. *Comparative Politics*. Dorsey, 1964.

Moreno, Frank J. and Rodman C. Rockefeller (eds.), "Social Research in Latin America," *The American Behavioral Scientist*, Vol. VII, No. 1 (September, 1964).

Russett, Bruce M. et al. *World Handbook of Political and Social Indicators*. Yale University Press. 1964.

Social Science Research Council, *Items*. Vol. 15, No. 2 (June, 1961); Vol. 16, No. 2 (June, 1962); Vol. 17, No. 2 (June, 1963); Vol. 18, No. 4 (December, 1964).

Social Science Research Council. Seminar Report. "Research in Comparative Politics," *American Political Science Review*, Vol. XLVII, No. 3 (September, 1953).

Wagley, Charles (ed.). *Social Science Research on Latin America*. Columbia University Press, 1964.

Ward, Robert E. et al. *Studying Politics Abroad*. Little, Brown, 1964.

BIBLIOGRAPHIES

American Political Science Review. Bibliographic sections, each issue.

American Universities Field Staff. *A Selected Bibliography: Asia, Africa, Eastern Europe, Latin America*. New York, 1960.

Blanksten, George I. "Bibliography on Latin American Politics and Government," *Inter-American Review of Bibliography*. Vol. IV, No. 3 (July-September, 1954).

Bowker Co., R.R. *1800 Books on Latin America*. New York, 1959.

Brown, Lyle C. *Latin America: A Bibliography*. (mimeo) Kingsville, Texas, 1962.

Gibson, Charles and E.V. Niemeyer. *Guide to the Hispanic American Historical Review*, 1946-1955. 1958.

Harrison, John P. *Guide to the Materials on Latin America in the National Archives*. Washington, 1961.

Hilton, Ronald. *Handbook of Hispanic Source Materials and Research Organizations in the United States*. 2nd Ed., 1956.

Kantor, Harry. *A Bibliography of Unpublished Doctoral Dissertations and Masters Theses Dealing with the Governments, Politics and International Relations of Latin America*. University of Florida, 1953.

Kidder, Frederick E., "Doctoral Dissertations in Latin American Area Studies, 1962-1963," *The Americas*, Vol. XXI, No. 2 (October, 1964).

Latin American Research Review. 1st number, Fall, 1965. Bibliographical articles and sections. Austin, Texas.

Pan-American Union. *Directory of Current Latin American Periodicals*. 1958.

_____. *Inter-American Review of Bibligraphy* (1951-)

_____. *Theses on Pan-American Topics*. Compiled by F.E. Kidder and A.D. Bushong. 1962.

U.S. Library of Congress. *A Bibliography of Latin American Bibliographies*.
_____. *A Guide to the Law and Legal Literature of*....(see appropriate country).

_____. *A Guide to the Official Publications of the Other American Republics*.

48

_____. *A List of the Latin American Periodicals Currently Received in the Library of Congress.*

UCLA. Center for Latin American Studies. *Guide to Latin American Studies.* 1966.

_____. *Latin America in Periodical Literature.* 1962-.

University of Florida. *Handbook of Latin American Studies.* 1937-.

DIRECTORIES, RESEARCH INVENTORIES

American Political Science Association. *Directory.* 1948, 1953, 1961.

American Political Science Review. September issues on dissertations.

Latin American Research Review. 1st number, Fall, 1965.

Library of Congress. Hispanic Foundation. *Directory of Latin Americanists.* 1966.

U.S. Department of State. Bureau of International Research. *External Research.*

University of California (Berkeley). Survey Research Center. International Data Library and Reference Service.

UCLA. Center for Latin American Studies. *A Master Directory for Latin America.* 1966.

University of Michigan. Survey Research Center. Inter-University Consortium for Political Research.

JOURNALS, REPORTS

American Academy of Political and Social Science. *Annals.*

American Anthropologist.

American Journal of Sociology.

American Political Science Review.

American Sociological Review.

American Universities Field Staff. *Reports.*

Americas.

The Americas.

Comparative Studies in Society and History.

Current History.

Foreign Affairs.

Hispanic-American Report.

Hispanic American Historical Review.

Inter-American Economic Affairs.

Journal of the History of Ideas.

Journal of Inter-American Studies.

Journal of Politics.

Midwest Journal of Political Science.

Pan American Union. *Bulletin.*

Political Science Quarterly.

Public Administration Review.

Public Opinion Quarterly.

Review of Politics.

Southwestern Social Science Quarterly.

Western Political Quarterly.

GENERAL REFERENCES

Busey, James L. *Latin American Political Guide.* (Annual)

Fitzgibbon, Russell H. *Constitutions of the Americas.* 1948.

Institute for the Comparative Study of Political Systems. (Various publications on electoral statistics).

Pan American Union. (Series on constitutions, republics, cities).

Russett, Alker, Lasswell, Deutsch. *World Handbook of Political and Social Indicators.* New Haven, 1964.

University of California (Los Angeles). *Statistical Abstract of Latin America.* (Annual)

POLITICS — GENERAL AND COMPARATIVE

Adams, Richard N. "Cultural Components of Central America," *American Anthropologist,* 58/5 (October, 1956).

_____. "Politics and Social Anthropology in Spanish America," *Human Organization,* Vol. 23 (Spring, 1964).

_____. *et al. Social Change in Latin America Today.* New York: Random House, 1961.

Adams, Richard N. and C.C. Cumberland. *United States' University Cooperation in Latin America*. East Lansing: Institute of Research on Overseas Programs, 1960.

Alexander, Robert J. *Communism in Latin America*. New Brunswick: Rutgers University Press, 1957.

_____. *Labor Movements in Latin America*. London: Gollancz, 1947.

_____. *Labor Relations in Argentina, Brazil and Chile*. New York: McGraw-Hill, 1962.

_____. *Prophets of Revolution: Profiles of Latin American Leaders*. New York: Macmillan, 1962.

Almond, Gabriel. "The Political Ideas of Christian Democracy," *Journal of Politics*, 10/4 (November, 1948).

Almond, Gabriel, and James S. Coleman. *The Politics of the Developing Areas*. Princeton: Princeton University Press, 1960.

Almond, Gabriel, and Sidney Verba. *The Civic Culture*. Princeton: Princeton University Press, 1963.

American Academy of Political and Social Science. "Latin America's Nationalistic Revolutions," *Annals*, Vol. 334 (March, 1961).

_____. "Mexico Today," *Annals*, Vol. 208 (March, 1940).

American Universities Field Staff. *Reports*. West Coast and East Coast South America Series.

Charles W. Anderson. "Central American Parties: A Functional Approach," *Western Political Quarterly*, 15/1 (March, 1962).

_____. "Politics and Development Policy in Central America," *Midwest Journal of Political Science*, 5/4 (November, 1961).

Arciniegas, German (ed.). *The Green Continent*. New York: Knopf, 1944.

_____. *The State of Latin America*. New York: Knopf, 1952.
_____. "What's Behind our Revolutions?" *Americas*, 1/1 (March, 1949).

Ardao, Arturo. "Positivism in Latin America," *Journal of the History of Ideas*, 24/4 (October-December, 1963).

Banks, Arthus S., and Robert B. Textor. *A Cross-Polity Survey*. Cambridge: M.I.T. Press, 1963.

Beals, Ralph L. "Social Stratification in Latin America," *American Journal of Sociology*, 58/4 (January, 1953).

Belaunde, Victor A. *Bolívar and the Political Thought of the Spanish American Revolution*. Baltimore: Johns Hopkins University Press, 1938.

Benham, F., and H.A. Holley. *A Short Introduction to the Economy of Latin America*. London: Oxford University Press, 1960.

Berle, Adolf A. *Latin America: Diplomacy and Reality*. New York: Harper and Row, 1962.

Bice, Hubert E., and Paul V. Horn. *Latin American Trade and Economics*. New York: Prentice-Hall, 1949.

Blanksten, George I. "Caudillismo in Northwestern South America," *South Atlantic Quarterly*, 51/4 (October, 1952).

———. "Political Groups in Latin America," *American Political Science Review*, 53/1 (March, 1959).

Bryce, James. *Modern Democracies*. 2 vols. New York: Macmillan, 1921.

———. *South America*. New York: Macmillan, 1912.

Busey, James L. "Central American Union: Latest Attempt," *Western Political Quarterly*, 14/1 (March, 1961).

———. "Foundations of Political Contrast: Costa Rica and Nicaragua," *Western Political Quarterly*, 11/3 (September, 1958).

———. *Latin America: Political Institutions and Processes*. New York: Random House, 1964.

Chapman, Charles E. "The Age of the Caudillos: A Chapter in Hispanic-American History," *Hispanic-American Historical Review*, 12/3 (August, 1932).

Chilcote, Ronald H. *The Press in Latin America, Spain and Portugal*. Stanford: Hispanic American Society, 1963.

Christensen, Asher N. *The Evolution of Latin American Government. A Book of Readings*. New York: Henry Holt, 1951.

Clagett, Helen L. *The Administration of Justice in Latin America*. New York: Oceana Publications, 1952.

Crawford, W. Rex. *A Century of Latin American Thought*. Cambridge: Harvard University Press, 1961. 2nd Ed.

Crow, John A. *The Epic of Latin America*. New York: Doubleday, 1946.

Davies, John Paton, Jr. *Foreign and Other Affairs. A View from the Radical Center*. New York: W.W. Norton, 1964.

Davis, Harold E. (ed.). *Government and Politics in Latin America.* New York: Ronald, 1958.

_____. *Latin American Leaders.* New York: H.W. Wilson, 1949.

_____. *Makers of Democracy in Latin America.* New York: H.W. Wilson, 1945.

_____. *Social Science Trends in Latin America.* Washington, D.C.: American University Press, 1950.

_____. "Trends in Social Thought in 20th Century Latin America," *Journal of Inter-American Studies,* 1/1 (January, 1959).

de Madariaga, Salvador. *Bolívar.* New York: Pellgrini and Cudahy, 1952.

_____. *Englishmen Frenchmen Spaniards. An Essay in Comparative Psychology.* London: Oxford University Press, 1937.

Deutsch, Karl W. *Nation-Building.* New York: Atherton, 1963.

_____. "Social Mobilization and Political Development," *American Political Science Review,* 55/3 (September, 1961).

Diffie, Bailey. "The Ideology of Hispanidad," *Hispanic-American Historical Review,* 23/3 (August, 1943).

Dozer, Donald M. *Are We Good Neighbors?* Gainesville: University of Florida Press, 1959.

_____. "Roots of Revolution in Latin America," *Foreign Affairs,* 27/2 (January, 1949).

Eder, Phanor J. *A Comparative Survey of Anglo-American and Latin-American Law.* New York: New York University Press, 1950.

Edelmann, Alexander T. *Latin American Government and Politics.* Homewood: Dorsey Press, 1965.

Eisenhower, Milton S. *The Wine Is Bitter.* New York: Doubleday, 1963.

Evans, Alona E. "The Colombian-Peruvian Asylum Case: The Practice of Diplomatic Asylum," *American Political Science Review,* 46/1 (March, 1952).

Fenwick, Charles G. *The Inter-American Regional System.* New York: Macmillan, 1949.

Fitzgibbon, Russell H. "Constitutional Development in Latin America: A Synthesis," *American Political Science Review,* 39/3 (June, 1945).

_____. *The Constitutions of the Americas.* Chicago: University of Chicago Press, 1948.

_____. "*Continuismo* in Central America and the Carribbean," *Inter-American Quarterly*, 2/3 (July, 1940).

_____. "Measurement of Latin-American Political Phenomena: A Statistical Experiment," *American Political Science Review*, 45/2 (June, 1951).

_____ "The Party Potpourri in Latin America," *Western Political Quarterly*, 10/1 (March, 1957).

_____. "The Process of Constitution Making in Latin America," *Comparative Studies in Society and History*, 3/1 (October, 1960).

_____. "A Statistical Evaluation of Latin American Democracy," *Western Political Quarterly*, 9/3 (September, 1956).

Fitzgibbon, Russell H., and Kenneth F. Johnson, "*Measurement of Latin American Political Change*," *American Political Science Review*, 55/3 (September, 1961).

Ford, Guy S. (ed.). *Dictatorships in the Modern World*. 2nd Ed. Minneapolis: University of Minnesota Press, 1939.

Furniss, Edgar S. "The United States, the Inter-American System and the U.N.," *Political Science Quarterly*, 65/3 (September, 1950).

García Calderón, Francisco. *Latin America: Its Rise and Progress*. London: Fisher Unwin, 1919.

Gil, Federico. "Cuatro Tendencias en la Política Latinoamericana," *Journal of Inter-American Studies*, 1/4 (October, 1959).

_____. "Responsible Parties in Latin America," *Journal of Politics*, 15/3 (August, 1953).

Gillin, John P. "Possible Cultural Maladjustments in Modern Latin America," *Journal of Inter-American Studies*, 5/2 (April, 1963).

Glade, William P. "Social Backwardness, Social Reform and Productivity in Latin America," *Inter-American Economic Affairs*, 15/3 (Winter, 1961).

Glick, Edward B. *Latin America and the Palestine Problem*. New York: Hertzl Foundation, 1958.

Gomez, R. A. *Government and Politics in Latin America*. Rev. Ed. New York: Random House, 1963.

_____. "Latin American Executives: Essence and Variations," *Journal of Inter-American Studies*, 3/1 (January, 1961).

Gordon, Wendell C. *The Political Economy of Latin America.* New York: Columbia University Press, 1965.

Graña, Cesar. "Cultural Nationalism: The Idea of Historical Destiny in Spanish America," *Social Research,* 29/4 (Winter, 1963).

Gunther, John. *Inside Latin America.* New York: Harpers, 1941.

Hamill, Hugh M. (ed.). *Dictatorship in Spanish America.* New York: Knopf, 1965.

Hanson, Simon G. *Economic Development in Latin America.* Washington, D. C.: Inter-American Affairs Press, 1951.

Haring, C. H. "Federalism in Latin America," in Conyers Read (ed.) *The Constitution Reconsidered.* New York: Columbia University Press, 1938.

Hirschman, Albert O. *Journeys Toward Progress: Studies of Economic Policy-Making in Latin America.* New York: 20th Century Fund, 1963.

_____. *Latin American Issues.* New York: 20th Century Fund, 1961.

Holmes, Olive. "Army Challenge in Latin America," *Foreign Policy Reports,* 25/14 (December, 1949).

Iutaka, Sugiyama. "Social Stratification Research in Latin America," *Latin American Research Review,* 1/1 (Fall, 1965).

James, Preston. *Latin America.* (Geography). New York: Odyssey, 1942.

Jane, Cecil. *Liberty and Despotism in Spanish America.* New York: Oxford University Press, 1929.

Johnson, John J. (ed). *Continuity and Change in Latin America.* Stanford: Stanford University Press, 1964.

_____. *Political Change in Latin America.* Stanford: Stanford University Press, 1958.

_____. (ed.). *Role of the Military in Underdeveloped Countries.* Princeton: Princeton University Press, 1962.

_____. *The Military and Society in Latin America.* Stanford: Stanford University Press, 1964.

Johnson, Kenneth F. "Causal Factors in Latin American Political Instability," *Western Political Quarterly,* 17/3 (September, 1964).

Jorrín, Miguel. *Governments of Latin America.* New York: Van Nostrand, 1953.

Kantor, Harry. "Los Partidos Populares de América Latina," *Journal of Inter-American Studies*, 6/2 (April, 1964).

Kling, Merle. "Taxes on the 'External' Sector; Index of Political Behavior in Latin America," *Midwest Journal of Political Science*, 3/2 (May, 1959).

_____. "Towards a Theory of Power and Political Instability in Latin America," *Western Political Quarterly*, 9/1 (March, 1956).

Kohn, Hans. *Nationalism*. New York: Van Nostrand, 1955.

Lauterbach, Albert. *Enterprise in Latin America: Business Attitudes in a Developing Economy*. Ithaca: Cornell University Press, 1965.

Leonard, Olen E., and Charles Loomis (eds.). *Readings in Latin American Social Organization and Institutions*. East Lansing: Michigan State College Press, 1953.

Lieuwen, Edwin. *Arms and Politics in Latin America*. New York: Praeger, 1960.

_____. "Changing Role of the Military in Latin America," *Journal of Inter-American Studies*, 3/4 (October, 1961).

_____. *Generals vs. Presidents: Neo-Militarism in Latin America*. New York: Praeger, 1964.

Linares Quintana, Segundo V. "Etiology of Revolutions in Latin America," *Western Political Quarterly*, 4/2 (June, 1951).

Lipset, Seymour M. "Democracy and Working-Class Authoritarianism," *American Sociological Review*, Vol. 24 (1959).

_____. *Political Man. The Social Bases of Politics*. New York: Doubleday, 1960.

Loewenstein, Karl. "The Presidency Outside the United States: A Study in Comparative Institutions," *Journal of Politics*, 11/3 (August, 1949).

Macdonald, A. F. *Latin American Politics and Government*. New York: Crowell, 1949.

Maddox, James G. *Technical Assistance by Religious Agencies in Latin America*. Chicago: University of Chicago Press, 1956.

Martz, John D. *Central America: The Crisis and the Challenge*. Chapel Hill: University of North Carolina Press, 1959.

_____. "Dilemmas in the Study of Latin American Politics," *Journal of Politics*, 26/3 (August, 1964).

_____. (ed.). *The Dynamics of Change in Latin American Politics.* Englewood Cliffs, N. J.: Prentice-Hall, 1965.

_____. "The Place of Latin America in the Study of Comparative politics," *Journal of Politics*, 28/1 (February, 1966).

May, Stacy and Galo Plaza Lasso. *The United Fruit Company in Latin America.* Washington, D. C.: National Planning Association, 1958.

McAlister, L. N. "Civil-Military Relations in Latin America," *Journal of Inter-American Studies*, 3/3 (July, 1961).

Mecham, J. Lloyd. *Church and State in Latin America.* Chapel Hill: University of North Carolina Press, 1934.

_____. "Democracy and Dictatorship in Latin America," *Southwestern Social Science Quarterly*, 41/3 (December, 1960).

_____. "Latin American Constitutions: Nominal and Real," *Journal of Politics*, 21/2 (May, 1959).

_____. *A Survey of United States-Latin American Relations.* Boston: Houghton-Mifflin, 1965.

Mehden, Fred von der, and Charles W. Anderson. "Political Action by the Military in the Developing Areas," *Social Research*, 28/4 (Winter, 1961).

Miliani, Domingo. "Utopian Socialism in Latin America," *Journal of the History of Ideas*, 24/4 (October-December,1963).

Millen, Bruce H. *The Political Role of Labor in Developing Countries.* Washington, D. C.: Brookings Institution, 1963.

Miró Quesada, Francisco. "Metaphysics and Latin American Ideology," *Journal of the History of Ideas*, 24/4 (October-December, 1963).

Mitchell, Harold. *Europe in the Caribbean.* Stanford: Hispanic American Society, 1963.

Moreno, Frank J. (ed.). "Social Research in Latin America," *American Behavioral Scientist*, 8/1 (September, 1964).

Morse, Richard M. "Latin American Cities: Aspects of Function and Structure," *Comparative Studies in Society and History*, 4/4 (July, 1962).

_____. "Urbanization in Latin America," *Latin American Research Review*, 1/1 (Fall, 1965).

_____. "Toward a Theory of Spanish American Government," *Journal of the History of Ideas*, 15/1 (January, 1954).

Naft, Stephen. "Fascism and Communism in South America," *Foreign Policy Association Report*, 13/19 (1937).

Nash, Manning. "The Multiple Society in Economic Development: Mexico and Guatemala," *American Anthropologist*, 59/5 (October, 1957).

Needler, Martin C. *Latin American Politics in Perspective*. New York: Van Nostrand, 1963.

_____. (ed.). *The Political Systems of Latin America*. New York: Van Nostrand, 1964.

Palmer, Thomas W., Jr. *Search for a Latin American Policy*. Gainesville: University of Florida Press, 1957.

Pendle, George. "Perón and Vargas," *Fortnightly Review*, Vol. 176 (n.s. 170), (November, 1951).

Pierson, W. W. (ed.). "The Pathology of Democracy in Latin America: A Symposium," *American Political Science Review*, 44/1 (March' 1950).

Pierson, W. W., and Federico Gil. *Governments of Latin America*. New York: McGraw-Hill, 1957.

Pike, Frederick B. "The Catholic Church in Central America," *Review of Politics*, 21/1 (January, 1959).

_____. (ed.). *The Conflict Between Church and State in Latin America*. New York: Knopf, 1964.

_____. (ed.). *Freedom and Reform in Latin America*. Notre Dame: Notre Dame Press, 1959.

_____. "Guatemala, the United States and Communism in the Americas," Review of Politics, 17/2 (April, 1955).

Plaza Lasso, Galo. *Problems of Democracy in Latin America*. Chapel Hill: University of North Carolina Press, 1955.

Poblete Troncoso, Moisés, and Ben G. Burnett "Latin American Labor Law: A Synthesis," *Inter-American Economic Affairs*, 12/2 (Autumn, 1958).

Puente, J. I. "The Nature and Powers of a 'De Facto' Government in Latin America," *Tulane Law Review*, Vol. 30 (1955).

Recasens, Luis, *et al. Latin-American Legal Philosophy*. Cambridge: Harvard University Press, 1948.

Ronning, C. Neale. "Intervention, International Law and the Inter-American System," *Journal of Inter-American Studies*, 3/2 (April, 1961).

____.*Law and Politics in Inter-American Diplomacy*. Rom. New York: John Wiley, 1963.

Rostow, W. W. *The Stages of Economic Growth*. Cambridge, England: Cambridge University Press, 1964.

Rowe, Leo S. "The Development of Democracy on the American Continent," *American Political Science Review*, 16/1 (February, 1922).

Russett, Bruce M., Hayward R. Alker, Karl W. Deutsch and Harold D. Lasswell. *World Handbook of Political and Social Indicators*. New Haven: Yale University Press, 1964.

Sanchez Reulet, Aníbal. *La Filosofía Latinoamericana Contemporánea*. Washington, D. C.: Pan American union, 1949.

Schaedel, Richard P. "Land Reform Studies," *Latin American Research Review*, 1/1 (Fall, 1965).

Schmitt, Karl M., and David Burks. *Evolution or Chaos: Dynamics of Latin American Government and Politics*. New York: Praeger, 1963.

Schulman, Sam. "Schema of Latin American Tenure Classes," *Southwestern Social Science Quarterly*, 37/2 (September, 1956).

Schurz, William L. *Latin America: A Descriptive Survey*. New York: E. P. Dutton, 1942.

_____. *This New World*. New York: E. P. Dutton, 1954.

Silvert, Kalman H. *Reaction and Revolution in Latin America: The Conflict Society*. New York: Hauser Press, 1961.

Simon, S. Fanny. "Anarchism and Anarcho-Syndicalism in South America," *Hispanic-American Historical Review*, 26/1 (February, 1946).

Smith, T. Lynn (ed.). *Agrarian Reform in Latin America*. New York: Knopf, 1965.

_____. "Current Population Trends in Latin America," *American Journal of Sociology*, 62/4 (January, 1957).

Spitz, David. *Patterns of Anti-Democratic Thought*. New York: Macmillan, 1949.

Stokes, William S. *Honduras: An Area Study in Government.* Madison: University of Wisconsin Press, 1950.

_____. *Latin American Politics.* New York: Crowell, 1959.

_____."Parliamentary Government in Latin America," *American Political Science Review*, 39/3 (June, 1945).

_____. "Violence as a Power Factor in Latin American Politics," *Western Political Quarterly*, 5/3 (September, 1952).

Stuart, Graham. *Latin America and the United States.* 4th Ed. New York: Appleton-Century, 1943.

Szulc, Tad. *The Winds of Revolution.* New York: Praeger, 1962.

Tannenbaum, Frank. "The Future of Democracy in Latin America," *Foreign Affairs* (April, 1955).

Tax, Sol, *et al. Heritage of Conquest: The Ethnology of Middle America.* Glencoe: Free Press, 1952.

_____. "The Problem of Democracy in Middle America," *American Sociological Review*, 10/2 (April, 1945).

Taylor, Philip B. "The Guatemalan Affair: A Critique of United States Foreign Policy," *American Political Science Review*, 50/3 (September, 1956).

Thomas, Ann Van Wynen, and A. J. Thomas. *The Organization of American States.* Dallas: Southern Methodist University Press, 1963.

Tuma, Elias H. "Agrarian Reform in Historical Perspective: A Comparative Study," *Comparative Studies in Society and History*, 6/1 (October, 1963).

United States Senate. Foreign Relations Subcommittee on American Republics. *United States — Latin American Relations.* 86th Congress, 2nd Session. Document 125. 1960.

University of Texas. Institute of Latin American Studies. *Intellectual Trends in Latin America.* Austin, 1945.

Veliz, Claudio (ed.). *Obstacles to Change in Latin America.* New York: Oxford, 1965.

Vivas, Eliseo. "The Spanish Heritage," *American Sociological Review*, 10/2 (April, 1945).

Wagley, Charles (ed.). *Social Science Research on Latin America.* New York: Columbia University Press, 1964.

Whitten, Norman E. "Power Structure and Sociocultural Change in Latin American Communities," *Social Forces*, 43/3 (March, 1965).

Wilgus, A. Curtis (ed.). *South American Dictators During the First Century of Independence*. Washington, D. C.: George Washington University Press, 1937.

Wyckoff, Theodore. "The Role of the Military in Latin American Politics," *Western Political Quarterly*, 13/3 (September, 1960).

Wythe, George. *Industry in Latin America*. New York: Columbia University Press, 1945.

Zea, Leopoldo (translated by P. P. Wiener). "History of Ideas in Latin America: Recent Works," *Journal of the History of Ideas*, 20/4 (October-December, 1959).

(translated by J. Abbott and L. Dunham). *The Latin American Mind*. Norman: University of Oklahoma Press, 1963.

POLITICS — ARGENTINA

Alexander, Robert J. *The Perón Era*. New York: Columbia University Press, 1951.

Amadeo, Santos P. *Argentine Constitutional Law*. New York: Columbia University Press, 1943.

Ayarragaray, Lucas. *La Anarquía Argentina y el Caudillismo*. Buenos Aires: L.J. Rosso, 1935.

Blanksten, George I. *Perón's Argentina*. Chicago: University of Chicago Press, 1953.

Burgin, Mirón. *The Economic Aspects of Argentine Federalism, 1820-1852*. Cambridge: Harvard University Press, 1946.

Cowles, Fleur. *Bloody Precedent*. New York: Random House, 1952.

Dunne, Peter M. "Church and State in Argentina," *Review of Politics*, 17/4 (October, 1945).

Easum, Donald B. "Justicialismo in Retrospect: Failure of the Peronista Time-Table," *Inter-American Economic Affairs*, 6/3 (Winter, 1952).

Gómez, R. A. "Intervention in Argentina: 1860-1930," *Inter-American Economic Affairs*, 1/3 (December, 1947).

Goodrich, Carter. "Argentina as a New Country," *Comparative Studies in Society and History*, 7/1 (October, 1964).

Hasbrouck, Alfred. "The Argentine Revolution of 1930," *Hispanic-American Historical Review*, 18/3 (August, 1938).

Ingenieros, José. *La Evolución de las Ideas Argentinas*. 2 vols. Buenos Aires: L. J. Rosso, 1918, 1920.

Kennedy, John J. *Catholicism, Nationalism and Democracy in Argentina*. Notre Dame: University of Notre Dame Press.

Kilgore, W. J. "Latin American Philosophy and the Place of Alejandro Korn," *Journal of Inter-American Studies*, 2/1 (January, 1960).

La Prensa, Editors of. *Defense of Freedom*. New York: John Day, 1952.

Linares Quintana, Segundo V. *Gobierno y Administración de la República Argentina*. 2 vols. Buenos Aires: Ed. Argentina, 1946.

_____. "The Development of Political Science in the Argentina Republic," *Contemporary Political Science* (UNESCO), 1950.

Macdonald, Austin F. *Government of the Argentine Republic*. New York: Crowell, 1942.

Millington, Thomas M. "President Arturo Illia and the Argentine Military," *Journal of Inter-American Studies*, 6/3 (July, 1964).

Neasham, V. Aubrey. "California's Influence on the Constitution of Argentina," *California Historical Society Quarterly*, 16/1 (1937).

Ortega y Gasset, José. "The Argentine State and the Argentinian" in *Toward a Philosophy of History*. New York: Norton, 1941.

Pendle, George. "Perón and Vargas," *Fortnightly Review*, Vol. 176 (n.s. 170), (November, 1951).

Potash, Robert A. "Argentina Political Parties: 1957-1958," *Journal of Inter-American Studies*, 1/4 (October, 1959).

_____. "The Changing Role of the Military in Argentina," *Journal of Inter-American Studies*, 3/4 (October, 1961).

Rennie, Ysabel F. *The Argentine Republic*. New York: Macmillan, 1945.

Romero, José. (translated by Thomas F. McGann). *A History of Argentine Political Thought*. Stanford: Stanford University Press, 1963.

Rowe, Leo S. *The Federal System of the Argentine Republic*. Washington, D. C.: Carnegie Institution, 1921.

Sánchez Viamonte, Carlos. *Historia Institucional de Argentina*. Mexico: Fondo de Cultura Economica, 1948.

62

Scobie, James R. *Argentina: A City and a Nation*. New York: Oxford, 1964.

Shuck, L. Edward. "Church and State in Argentina," *Western Political Quarterly*, 2/4 (December, 1949).

Snow, Peter. "Argentina Radicalism, 1957-63," *Journal of Inter-American Studies*, 5/4 (October, 1963).

_____. "Parties and Politics in Argentina: The Elections of 1962 and 1963," *Midwest Journal of Political Science*, 9/1 (February 1965).

Taylor, Carl C. *Rural Life in Argentina*. Baton Rouge: Louisiana State University Press, 1948.

White, John W. *Argentina: The Life Story of a Nation*. New York: Viking Press, 1942.

POLITICS — BOLIVIA

Alexander, Robert J. *The Bolivian National Revolution*. New Brunswick: Rutgers University Press, 1958.

Arnade, Charles W. "Bolivia's Social Revolution, 1952-59: A Discussion of Sources," *Journal of Inter-American Studies*, 1/3 (July, 1959).

Leonard, Olen E. *Bolivia: Land, People and Institutions*. Washington, D. C.: Scarecrow Press, 1952.

_____. "La Paz, Bolivia: Its Population and Growth," *American Sociological Review*, 13/4 (August, 1948).

Martin, Lois D. *Bolivia in 1956*. Stanford: Hispanic American Report, 1958.

Patch, Richard W. (Various reports as correspondent for American Universities Field Staff, 1958-).

POLITICS — BRAZIL

Cruz Costa, João. *A History of Ideas in Brazil*. Berkeley: University of California Press, 1964.

Cunha, Euclides de. *Rebellion in the Backlands*. Chicago: University of Chicago Press, 1944.

Dos Passos, John. *Brazil on the Move*. New York: Doubleday, 1963.

Freyre, Gilberto. (translated by Harriet de Onis). *The Mansions and the Shanties*. New York: Knopf, 1963.

Furtado, Celso. *The Economic Growth of Brazil*. Berkeley: University of California Press, 1963.

Gordon, Lincoln. *United States Manufacturing Investment in Brazil*. Cambridge: Harvard Business School, 1962.

Hambloch, Ernest. *His Majesty the President of Brazil*. New York: E. P. Dutton, 1936.

Harris, Marvin. *Town and Country in Brazil*. New York: Columbia University Press, 1956.

Hill, Lawrence F. (ed.). *Brazil*. Berkeley: University of California Press, 1947.

Hunnicut, Benjamin H. *Brazil: World Frontier*. New York: Van Nostrand, 1949.

Lipson, L. "Government in Contemporary Brazil," *Canadian Journal of Economics and Political Science* (May, 1956).

Loewenstein, Karl. *Brazil Under Vargas*. New York: Macmillan, 1942.

Martin, Percy A. "Federalism in Brazil," *Hispanic-American Historical Review*, 18/2 (November, 1938).

Morse, Richard M. *From Community to Metropolis: A Biography of Sao Paulo, Brazil*. Gainesville: University of Florida Press, 1958.

Pendle, George. "Perón and Vargas," *Fortnightly Review*, Vol. 176 (n.s. 170), (November, 1952).

Reining, Henry. "The Brazilian Program of Administrative Reform," *American Political Science Review*, 39/3 (June, 1945).

Ribeiro, René. "On the *Amaziado* Relationship, and Other Aspects of the Family in Recife," *American Sociological Review*, 10/1 (February, 1945).

Robock, Stefan H. *Brazil's Developing Northeast*. Washington, D. C.: Brookings Institution, 1963.

Rosen, Bernard C. "Socialization and Achievement Motivation in Brazil," *American Sociological Review*, 27/4 (August, 1962).

Smith, T. Lynn. *Brazil: People and Institutions*. 3rd Ed. Baton Rouge: Louisiana State University Press, 1963.

————. "Patterns of Living in the U. S. and Brazil; A Comparison," *Journal of Inter-American Studies*, 3/2 (April, 1961).

Wagley, Charles. *An Introduction to Brazil*. New York: Columbia University Press, 1963.

————. (ed.). *Race and Class in Rural Brazil*. Paris: UNESCO, 1952.

Wyckoff, Theodore, "Brazilian Political Parties," *South Atlantic Quarterly*, Vol. 56 (1957).

Young, Jordan M. "The Brazilian Congressional Elections," *Journal of Inter-American Studies* 5/1 (January, 1963).

_____. "Some Permanent Characteristics of Contemporary Brazil," *Journal of Inter-American Studies*, 6/3 (July, 1964).

POLITICS — CHILE

Abbott, Roger S. "The Role of Contemporary Political Parties in Chile," *American Political Science Review*, 45/2 (June, 1951).

Blasier, S. Cole. "Chile: A Communist Battleground," *Political Science Quarterly*, 65/3 (September, 1950).

Bonilla, Frank. "The Student Federation of Chile: 50 Years of Political Action," *Journal of Inter-American Studies*, 2/3 (July, 1960).

Butland, Gilbert J. *Chile: An Outline of Its Geography, Economics and Politics.* London: Royal Institute of International Affairs, 1951.

Cruz Coke, Ricardo. *Geografía Electoral de Chile.* Santiago: Ed. del Pacifico, 1952.

Donoso, Ricardo. *Las Ideas Políticas en Chile.* Mexico: Fondo de Cultura Economica, 1946.

Gil, Federico G. *The Political System of Chile.* Boston: Houghton-Mifflin, 1966.

Holmes, Olive. "Chile: Microcosm of Modern Conflicts," *Foreign Policy Report*, Vol. 15 (July, 1946).

Loewenstein, Karl. "Legislation for the Defense of the State in Chile," *Columbia Law Review*, 44/3 (May, 1944).

McBride, G. M. *Chile: Land and Society.* New York: American Geographic Society, 1936.

Pike, Frederick B. "Chilean Class Relations, 1850-1960," *Hispanic-American Historical Review*, 43/1 (February, 1963).

Pike, Frederick B., and Donald W. Bray, "Vista of Catastrophe: U.S. — Chilean Relations," *Review of Politics*, 22/3 (July, 1960).

Stevenson, John R. *The Chilean Popular Front.* Philadelphia: University of Pennsylvania Press, 1942.

Thomas, Jack R. "The Socialist Republic of Chile," *Journal of Inter-American Studies*, 4/2 (April, 1964).

POLITICS — COLOMBIA

Caldwell, Lynton K. "Technical Assistance and Administrative Reform in Colombia," *American Political Science Review*, 47/2 (June, 1953).

Fluharty, Vernon L. *Dance of the Millions: Military Rule and the Social Revolution in Colombia, 1930-1956*. Pittsburgh: University of Pittsburgh Press, 1957.

Gibson, William M. *The Constitutions of Colombia*. Durham: Duke University Press, 1948.

Johnson, Kenneth F. "Political Radicalism in Colombia: Electoral Dynamics of 1962 and 1964," *Journal of Inter-American Studies*, 7/1 (January, 1965).

Martz, John D. *Colombia: A Contemporary Political Survey*. Chapel Hill: University of North Carolina Press, 1962.

Schmid, Peter, "Saints, Sinners, and Civil War," *American Mercury*, 75/3 (September, 1952).

Williamson, Robert C. "Toward a Theory of Political Violence: The Case of Rural Colombia," *Western Political Quarterly*, 18/1 (March, 1965).

POLITICS — COSTA RICA

Biesanz, John and Mavis. *Costa Rican Life*. New York: Columbia University Press, 1944.

Busey, James L. "Foundations of Political Contrast: Costa Rica and Nicaragua," *Western Political Quarterly*, 11/3 (September, 1958).
——— . *Notes on Costa Rican Democracy*. Boulder: University of Colorado Press, 1962.

Kantor, Harry. *The Costa Rican Elections of 1953*. Gainesville: University of Florida Press, 1958.

Loomis, Charles P., and John McKinney. "Systemic Differences Between Latin-American Communities of Family Farms and Large Estates," *American Journal of Sociology*, 61/5 (March, 1956).

POLITICS — CUBA

(Omitted due to obvious difficulties in assessing the Cuban revolution).

POLITICS — DOMINICAN REPUBLIC

Galíndez, Jesús de. *La Era de Trujillo*. Buenos Aires: Ed. Americana, 1956.

POLITICS — ECUADOR

Blanksten, George I. *Ecuador: Constitutions and Caudillos*. Los Angeles: University of California Press, 1951.

POLITICS — GUATEMALA

Arevalo, Juan José. *Escritos Politicos*. Guatemala: Tip. Nacional, 1945.

Bush, Archer C. *Organized Labor in Guatemala, 1944-1949*. Hamilton, N. Y.: Colgate University Area studies, 1950.

Gillin, John. "Race Relations Without Conflict: A Guatemalan Town," *American Journal of Sociology*, 53/5 (March, 1948).

Schneider, Ronald M. *Communism in Guatemala, 1944-1954*. New York: Praeger, 1958.

Silvert, Kalman H. *A Study in Government: Guatemala. Part I*. New Orleans: Tulane University, 1954.

————. *A Study in Government: Guatemala. Part II*. New Orleans: Tulane University, 1956.

Tax, Sol. *Penny Capitalism: A Guatemalan Indian Economy*. Washington, D.C.: Government Printing Office, 1953.

Taylor, Philip B. "The Guatemalan Affair: A Critique of United States Foreign Policy," *American Political Science Review*, 50/3 (September, 1956).

Tumin, Melvin M. "Reciprocity and Stability of Caste in Guatemala," *American Sociological Review*, 14/1 (February, 1949).

U. S. Department of State. *A Case History of Communist Penetration*. Publ. #6465: Inter-American Series, 1957.

Ydígoras Fuentes, Miguel. *My War With Communism*. New York: Prentice-Hall, 1963.

POLITICS — HAITI

DeYoung, Maurice. *Man and Land in the Haitian Economy*, Gainesville: University of Florida Press, 1958.

POLITICS — HONDURAS

Checchi, Vincent *et al. Honduras: A Problem in Economic Development.* New York: 20th Century Fund, 1959.

Stokes, William S. *Honduras: An Area Study in Government.* Madison: University of Wisconsin Press, 1950.

POLITICS — MEXICO

Alisky, Marvin. *The Governors of Mexico.* El Paso: Texas Western College, 1965.

————. *State and Local Government in Sonora, Mexico.* Tempe: Arizona State University, 1962.

Almond, Gabriel and Sidney Verba. *The Civic Culture.* Princeton: Princeton University Press, 1963.

Bermúdez, Antonio J. *The Mexican National Petroleum Industry.* Stanford: Hispanic-American Report, 1963.

Brandenburg, Frank. *The Making of Modern Mexico.* Englewood Cliffs, N. J.: Prentice-Hall, 1964.

————. "Organized Business in Mexico," *Inter-American Economic Affairs, 12/3* (Winter, 1958).

Cárdenas, Leonard. *The Municipality in Northern Mexico.* El Paso: Texas Western College, 1963.

Clapp, Orrin E. "Mexican Social Types," *American Journal of Sociology, 69/4* (January, 1964).

Clark, Marjorie R. *Organized Labor in Mexico.* Chapel Hill: University of North Carolina Press, 1934.

Cline, Howard F. *Mexico: Revolution to Evolution: 1940-1960.* New York: Oxford, 1963.

Cumberland, Charles C. *Mexican Revolution: Genesis Under Madero.* Austin: University of Texas Press, 1952.

Dotson, Floyd. "A Note on Participation in Voluntary Associations in a Mexican City," *American Sociological Review, 18/4* (August, 1953).

Ebenstein, William. "Public Administration in Mexico," *Public Administration Review, 5/2* (Spring, 1945).

Flower, Elizabeth. "Mexican Revolt Against Positivism," *Journal of the History of Ideas, 10/1* (January, 1949).

Garza, David T. "Factionalism in the Mexican Left: The Frustration of the MLR," *Western Political Quarterly, 17/3* (September, 1964).

Glade, William P., and Charles W. Anderson. *The Political Economy of Mexico: Two Studies*. Madison: University of Wisconsin Press, 1963.

Gruening, Ernest. *Mexico and Its Heritage*. New York: Century, 1928.

Gumpel, Henry J., and Hugo B. Margain. *Taxation in Mexico*. Boston: Little, Brown, 1957.

Hancock, Richard. *The Role of the Bracero in the Economic and Cultural Dynamics of Mexico*. Stanford: Hispanic American Society, 1959.

Humphrey, Norman D. "Social Stratification in a Mexican Town," *Southwestern Journal of Anthropology, 5/2* (Summer, 1949).

Johnson, Kenneth F. "Ideological Correlates of Right Wing Political Alienation in Mexico," *American Political Science Review, 59/3* (September, 1965).

Kling, Merle. *A Mexican Interest Group in Action*. Englewood Cliffs, N.J.: Prentice-Hall, 1961.

Lewis, Oscar. *Life in a Mexican Village: Tepoztlán Revisited*. Urbana: University of Illinois Press, 1951.

Macfarland, Charles S. *Chaos in Mexico: The Conflict of Church and State*. New York: Harper Bros., 1935.

Mecham, J. Lloyd. "An Appraisal of the Revolution in Mexico," in A. C. Wilgus (ed.). *The Caribbean at Mid-Century*. Gainesville: University of Florida Press, 1951.

Morton, Ward M. *Woman Suffrage in Mexico*. Gainesville: University of Florida Press, 1963.

Padgett, L. Vincent. "Mexico's One-Party System: A Re-evaluation," *American Political Science Review, 51/4* (December, 1957).

Padgett, L. Vincent and Orrin E. Clapp. "Power Structure and Decision-Making in a Mexican Border City," *American Journal of Sociology, 65/4* (January, 1960).

Ramos, Samuel. *Historia de la Filosofía en México*. México: Imp. Universitaria, 1943.

———. (translated by P. G. Earle). *Profile of Man and Culture in Mexico*. Austin: University of Texas Press, 1965.

Romanell, Patrick. *The Making of the Mexican Mind*. Lincoln: University of Nebraska Press, 1952.

Sánchez, George I. *Mexico: A Revolution by Education*. New York: 1936.

Schmitt, Karl M. *Communism in Mexico: A Study in Political Frustration*. Austin: University of Texas Press, 1965.

––––––. "Communism in Mexico Today," *Western Political Quarterly*, 15/1 (March, 1962).

Scott, Robert E. "Budget-Making in Mexico," *Inter-American Economic Affairs*, 9/2 (Autumn, 1955).

––––––. *Mexican Government in Transition*. Urbana: University of Illinois Press, 1959.

Senior, Clarence. *Land Reform and Democracy*. Gainesville: University of Florida Press, 1959.

Sierra, Justo, *Evolución Política del Pueblo Mexicano*. Mexico: University Nac. Auton. de Mexico, 1948.

Silva Herzog, Jesús. *Un Ensayo Sobre la Revolución Mexicana*. Mexico: Cuadernos Americanos, 1946.

Simpson, Eyler N. *The Ejido: Mexico's Way Out*. Chapel Hill: University of North Carolina Press, 1937.

Spain, Auguste O. "Mexican Federalism Revisited," *Western Political Quarterly*, 9/3 (September, 1956).

Stabb, Martin S. "Indigenism and Racism in Mexican Thought: 1857-1911," *Journal of Inter-American Studies*, 1/4 (October, 1959).

Tannenbaum, Frank. *Mexican Agrarian Revolution*. New York: Macmillan, 1929.

––––––. *Mexico: The Struggle for Peace and Bread*. New York: Knopf, 1950.

––––––. "Personal Government in Mexico," *Foreign Affairs*, 27/1 (October, 1948).

Taylor, Philip B. "The Mexican Elections of 1958: Affirmation of Authoritarianism," *Western Political Quarterly*, 13/1 (September, 1960).

Tinney, E. L., and J. E. Conley. "On Political Modernity in Mexico: Consensus and Recruitment," *Southwestern Social Science Quarterly*, 44/3 (December, 1963).

Tucker, William P. *Mexican Government Today*. Minneapolis: University of Minnesota Press, 1957.

Vernon, Raymond. *The Dilemma of Mexico's Development*. Cambridge: Harvard University Press, 1963.

Whetten, Nathan L. *Rural Mexico*. Chicago: University of Chicago Press, 1948.

POLITICS — NICARAGUA

Busey, James L. "Foundations of Political Contrast: Costa Rica and Nicaragua," *Western Political Quarterly*, 11/3 (September, 1958).

POLITICS — PANAMA

Biesanz, John, and Luke M. Smith. "Panamanian Politics," *Journal of Politics*, 14/3 (August, 1952).

————. "Race Relations in Panama and the Canal Zone," *American Journal of Sociology*, 57/1 (July, 1951).

Goldrich, Daniel. "Panamanian Students Orientations Toward Government and Democracy," *Journal of Inter-American Studies*, 5/3 (July, 1963).

Goldrich, Daniel, and Edward W. Scott. "Developing Political Orientations of Panamanian Students." *Journal of Politics*, 23/1 (February, 1961).

POLITICS — PERU

Chang-Rodríguez, Eugenió. *La Literatura Política de González Práda, Maríategui y Haya de la Torre*, Mexico: Ed. de Andrea, 1957.

Dobyns, Henry F. *The Social Matrix of Peruvian Indigenous Communities. Ithaca:* Cornell University, 1964.

Evans, Alone E. "The Colombian-Peruvian Asylum Case: The Practice of Diplomatic Asylum," *American Political Science Review*, 46/1 (March, 1952).

Ford, T.R. *Man and Land in Peru*. Gainesville: University of Florida Press, 1955.

García Calderón, Francisco *Le Perou Contemporaine: Etude Sociale*, Paris: Dujarric, 1907.

Gillin, John P. *Moche, A Peruvian Coastal Community*, Washington, D.C.: Government Printing Office, 1947.

Gomez, R.A. "Peru: The Politics of Military Guardianship," in Martin Needler (ed.). *The Political Systems of Latin America.* New York: Van Nostrand, 1964.

Kantor, Harry. *The Ideology and Program of the Peruvian Aprista Party,* Los Angeles: University of California Press, 1953.

———. "The Aprista Search for a Program Applicable to Latin America," *Western Political Quarterly,* 5/4 (December, 1952).

McNicoll, Robert E. "Recent Political Developments in Peru," *Inter-American Economic Affairs,* 18/1 (Summer, 1964).

Needler, Martin C. "Cabinet Responsibility in a Presidential System: The Case of Peru," *Parliamentary Affairs,* 18/2 (Spring, 1965).

Patch, Richard W. (Various reports as correspondent for American Universities Field Staff, 1958-).

Payne, James L. *Labor and Politics in Peru.* New Haven: Yale University Press, 1965.

Pike, Frederick B. "The Modernized Church in Peru: Two Aspects." *Review of Politics,* 26/3 (July, 1964).

———. "The Old and the New APRA in Peru: Myth and Reality," *Inter-American Economic Affairs,* 18/2 (Autumn, 1964).

POLITICS — URUGUAY

Fitzgibbon, Russell H. "Adoption of a Collegiate Executive in Uruguay," *Journal of Politics,* 14/4 (November, 1952).

———. *Uruguay: Portrait of a Democracy.* New Brunswick, N.J.: Rutgers University Press, 1954.

Hanson, Simon G. *Utopia in Uruguay.* New York: Oxford, 1938.

Kitchen, James D. "National Personnel Administration in Uruguay," *Inter-American Economic Affairs,* 4/1 (Summer, 1950).

Pendle, George. *Uruguay, South America's First Welfare State.* London: Royal Institute of International Affairs, 1952.

Taylor, Philip B. *The Executive Power in Uruguay.* Berkeley: University of California Press, 1951.

———. "Electoral System in Uruguay," *Journal of Politics,* 17/1 (February, 1955).

————. *Government and Politics of Uruguay*. New Orleans: Tulane University Press, 1960.

————. "Interests and Institutional Dysfunction in Uruguay," *American Political Science Review*, 57/1 (March 1963).

————. "Interparty Cooperation and Uruguay's 1952 Constitution," *Western Political Quarterly*, 7/3 (September, 1954).

Vanger, Milton I. *José Battle Ordoñez of Uruguay*. Cambridge: Harvard University Press, 1963.

————. "Uruguay Introduces Government by Committee," *American Political Science Review*, 48/2 (June, 1954).

POLITICS — VENEZUELA

Griffin, Charles C. "Regionalism's Role in Venezuelan Politics," *Inter-American Quarterly*, 3/4 (October, 1941).

Kantor, Harry, "The Development of *Acción Democrática de Venezuela*," *Journal of Inter-American Studies*, 1/2 (March, 1959).

Lieuwen, Edwin. *Petroleum in Venezuela*. Berkeley: University of California Press, 1954.

————. *Venezuela*. New York: Oxford, 1961.

Lott, Leo B. "Executive Power in Venezuela," *American Political Science Review*, 50/2 (June, 1956).

————. "Nationalization of Justice in Venezuela," *Inter-American Economic Affairs*, 13/1 (Summer, 1959).

————. "The 1952 Venezuelan Elections: A Lesson for 1957," *Western Political Quarterly*, 10/3 (September, 1957).

Martz, John D. *Acción Democrática: Evolution of a Modern Political Party in Venezuela*, Princeton: Princeton University Press, 1966.

————. "Venezuela's Generation of '28': the Genesis of Political Democracy," *Journal of Inter-American Studies*, 6/1 (January, 1964).

Tugwell, Franklin. "The Christian Democrats of Venezuela," *Journal of Inter-American Studies*, 7/2 (April, 1965).

Vallenilla Lanz, Laureano. *Cesarismo Democrático*, Caracas, 1929.

Wilgus, A.C. (ed.). *The Caribbean: Venezuelan Development*. Gainesville: University of Florida Press, 1963.

75

INSTITUTE OF GOVERNMENT RESEARCH
PUBLICATION SERIES

American Government Studies

1. The Role of Political Parties in Congress: A Bibliography and
   Research Guide
   Charles Jones and Randall B. Ripley, 1966. $1.50

2. The Politics of Food for Peace: Executive-Legislative Interaction
   Peter A. Toma, 1967.   Hardbound $3.95

Arizona Government Studies

1. State Budget Preparation in Arizona
   Paul Kelso, 1964. $1.50

2. Vox Populi: The Battle of 103
   Robert E. Riggs, 1964. $1.50

3. Politics and Legislation: The Office of Governor in Arizona
   Roy D. Morey, 1965.   Hardbound $4.00

4. The Movement for Administrative Reorganization in Arizona
   Robert E. Riggs, 1964. $1.50

Comparative Government Studies

1. Relations of the Profumo Rebels With Their Local Parties
   Jorgen B. Rasmussen, 1966. $1.50

2. The Study of Latin American Politics in University Programs
   in the United States
   R. A. Gomez, 1967. $1.50

International Studies

1. Cold War Diplomacy: The Impact of International Conflicts
   on Diplomatic Communications and Travel
   Clifton E. Wilson, 1966. $1.50